Selected Poems

By Richard Hugo

A Run of Jacks

Death of the Kapowsin Tavern

Good Luck in Cracked Italian

The Lady in Kicking Horse Reservoir

What Thou Lovest Well Remains American

31 Letters and 13 Dreams

The Triggering Town
Lectures and Essays on Poetry and Writing

White Center

Selected Poems

Making Certain it Goes On
The Collected Poems of Richard Hugo

The Real West Marginal Way
A Poet's Autobiography

Selected Poems

Richard Hugo

W · W · NORTON & COMPANY

New York · London

W. W. Norton & Company, Inc., 500 Fifth Avenue, New York, NY 10110
W. W. Norton & Company Ltd, 10 Coptic Street, London WC1A 1PU

Copyright © 1979, 1977, 1975, 1973 by W. W. Norton & Company
Printed in the United States of America.

Library of Congress Cataloging in Publication Data

Hugo, Richard F
  Selected poems.

PS3515.U3A17   1979   811'.5'4   79-11714
ISBN 0-393-00936-X
      8 9 0

For my colleagues
in creative writing at Montana

Madeline DeFrees
Earl Ganz
Bill Kittredge

Contents

from *Good Luck in Cracked Italian* (1969)

from *The Lady in Kicking Horse Reservoir* (1973)

from *What Thou Lovest Well Remains American* (1975)

from *31 Letters and 13 Dreams* (1977)

from *A Run of Jacks* (1961)

Trout

Quick and yet he moves like silt.
I envy dreams that see his curving
silver in the weeds. When stiff as snags
he blends with certain stones.
When evening pulls the ceiling tight
across his back he leaps for bugs.

I wedged hard water to validate his skin—
call it chrome, say red is on
his side like apples in a fog, gold
gills. Swirls always looked one way
until he carved the water into many
kinds of current with his nerve-edged nose.

And I have stared at steelhead teeth
to know him, savage in his sea-run growth,
to drug his facts, catalog his fins
with wings and arms, to bleach the black
back of the first I saw and frame the cries
that sent him snaking to oblivions of cress.

Near Kalalock

Throw sand dollars and they sail alive.
One dead salmon slides to immediate maggots
and the long starch of his side begins,
the chunk of belly gone in teeth
beyond the sonar stab, in green too thick
for signals from our eyes. Tan foam tumbles
and we call the bourbon in us wind.

We put this day in detent with a pastoral
anxiety for stars. Remember when our eyes
were ocean floors and the sun was dissonant
and cold, unlike today. Scream at waves
go back you fools or die, and say once
light was locked in a horizoned hunger.

A crack wind breaks the driftwood's white
from stark to cream. East is lost
but serious with lines: defeated slant
of grass, the cirrus pointed and the sudden
point of sun, the lean of ocean
on our throats, bacon-baited knocks
of sea perch in our palms.

Now the shore is speared by ancient orange,
let a trickle say a beach is bleeding.
Tonight the sea will come like the eyes
of all cats in the world stampeding.

West Marginal Way

One tug pounds to haul an afternoon
of logs up river. The shade
of Pigeon Hill across the bulges
in the concrete crawls on reeds
in a short field, cools a pier
and the violence of young men
after cod. The crackpot chapel,
with a sign erased by rain, returned
before to calm and a mossed roof.

A dim wind blows the roses
growing where they please. Lawns
are wild and lots are undefined
as if the payment made in cash
were counted then and there.

These names on boxes will return
with salmon money in the fall,
come drunk down the cinder arrow
of a trail, past the store of Popich,
sawdust piles and the saw mill
bombing air with optimistic sparks,
blinding gravel pits and the brickyard
baking, to wives who taught themselves
the casual thirst of many summers
wet in heat and taken by the sea.

Some places are forever afternoon.
Across the road and a short field
there is the river, split and yellow
and this far down affected by the tide.

La Push

Fish swim onto sand in error.
Birds need only the usual wind
to be fanatic, no bright orange
or strange names. Waves fall
from what had been flat water,
and a child sells herring
crudely at your door.

The store has a candy turnover
amazing to the proprietor.
He expected when he came
a Nordic rawness, serrated shore,
a broken moon, artifacts
and silence, large sales of corn.

Smelt are trapped in the river
by a summer habit, limit
of old netting rights ignored.
Who but an officed lawyer
far away has read the treaty,
his sense of rightness rounded
in a bar? The broker's pier
is measuring the day in kings and jacks.

Your land ends at this border,
water and stone, mobile in tide,
diffuse in storm, but here.

The final fist of island rock
does not strike space away. Swim
and you are not in your country.

Back of Gino's Place

Most neglect this road, the concrete torn
and hunched, purple boxcars
roasting in the wind or in the sun,
both direct as brass. Only smoke
from two shacks and a scratchy radio
prevent abandonment from falling
on this lateral bare area like fog.

In the winter what clean nightmare
brought a sketcher here
to risk his hands, the loss of line
in this much light? Not the poverty
alone, but other ways of being,
using basic heat: wood brought in
by the same sea that is blaring
wealthy ships to a freshly painted port.

He was right to come. Light
in this place cannot kill the lines
of the charred boat, the rusted net,
the log-boom beached and slanted
waiting for a tide. Not when a need to die
here, just to be an unobtrusive ghost,
takes from mud and wood the color of the day.

Ballad of the Upper Bumping

In the pounding white is a man to kill,
vague in spray, hidden under the fall,
aware of roots convenient for descent
and the intentional guns,
and gone like cones in the pour
before the gunners can aim.

Easily the gunners' coming has a core.
Here was a castoff widely hunted king
convinced these commoners would not climb down
shale scared gray by the roar.
They see him clawing moss spun out in foam
and the fern snap off in his hand.

The river screams release from run-off snow.
His plunge converted to the natural
by glacial green and the blurred bed
magnified in May.
He thought the kingdom waters loyal,
and rivers know where royalty can go.

Hermits dance the news to jubilant cities.
Leaders shout he will be found in August
blue where dollys spawn.
His gems will glow outrageous in the pool
like teeth reported in his smile;
our queen turned slightly from the flogger's jest.

The king is dead. Long dance the queen
with a withering hermit down the streets
where gunners return to some girls.
Kisses sting at stories of the gorge,
roots that held in slipping shale,
the gun-impounding roar.

Water strands relax and water fades
from hands and moving water needs
old noises like the hum
of rats in stranded silt.
The river void of noise, the silent
whitefish slip to sucker colored rocks.

Pools are scanned by the paid incisive eyes
of camping children, every riffle checked,
each log and large stone poked
and no king turned.
Now absolutist beavers clog the stream
and every ponderosa hides a breathing king.

A poet said the force of flowing years
beat those noble bones to a petty size
to string them with the normal skeletons
of autumn on the sand.
Look. Today we call these salmon kings.
He was hanged for gross imagining.

Gunners see him every May in the white,
and never seeing him, shoot through rainbowing spray.
Gone like cones in the pour—
and what can the gunners say.
The queen is thin in a cave removed from summer.
And wet light rolls through the hermit sleep of a hunter.

Skykomish River Running

Aware that summer baked the water clear,
today I came to see a fleet of trout.
But as I wade the salmon limp away,
their dorsal fins like gravestones in the air,
on their sides the red that kills the leaves.
Only sun can beat a stream this thin.
The river Sky is humming in my ear.

Where this river empties in the sea,
trout are waiting for September rain
to sting their thirst alive. If they speed
upstream behind the kings and eat the eggs
the silvers lay, I'll pound the drum for rain.
But sunlight drums, the river is the same,
running like old water in my ear.

I will cultivate the trout, teach their fins
to wave in water like the legs of girls
tormented black in pools. I will swim
a week to be a witness to the spawning,
be a trout, eat the eggs of salmon—
anything to live until the trout and rain
are running in the river in my ear.

The river Sky is running in my hair.
I am floating past the troutless pools
learning water is the easy way to go.
I will reach the sea before December

when the Sky is turning gray and wild
and rolling heavy from the east to say
late autumn was an Oriental child.

1614 Boren

Room on room, we poke debris for fun,
chips of dolls, the union picnic flag,
a valentine with a plump girl in a swing
who never could grow body hair or old
in all that lace (her flesh the color
of a salmon egg), a black-edged scroll
regretting death: "whereas—Great Architect—
has seen it fit—the lesser aerie here—
great aerie in the sky—deep sympathy."
Someone could have hated this so much . . .
he owns a million acres in Peru.

What does the picture mean, hung where it is
in the best room? Peace, perhaps. The calm road
leading to the house half hid by poplars,
willows and the corny vines bad sketchers used
around that time, the white canal in front
with two innocuous boats en route,
the sea suggested just beyond the bar,
the world of harm behind the dormant hill.

Why could room 5 cook and 7 not?
These dirty rooms were dirty even then,
the toilets ancient when installed,
and light was always weak and flat
like now, or stark from a bare bulb.
And the boarders when they spoke of this
used "place" and "house," the one with photos

of Alaska on his wall said "edifice."
This home could be a joke on the horizon—
bad proportions and the color of disease.

But the picture, where? The Netherlands
perhaps. There are Netherland canals.
But are they bleached by sky, or scorched
pale gray by an invader's guns?
It can't exist. It's just a sketcher's whim.
The world has poison and the world has sperm
and water looks like water, not like milk
or a cotton highway. There's a chance
a man who sweated years in a stale room,
probably one upstairs, left the picture here
on purpose, and when he moved believed
that was the place he was really moving from.

Neighbor

The drunk who lives across the street from us
fell in our garden, on the beet patch
yesterday. So polite. Pardon me,
he said. He had to be helped up and held,
steered home and put to bed, declaring
we got to have another drink and smile.

I admit my envy. I've found him in salal
and flat on his face in lettuce, and bent
and snoring by that thick stump full of rain
we used to sail destroyers on.
And I've carried him home so often
stone to the rain and me, and cheerful.

I try to guess what's in that dim warm mind.
Does he think about horizoned firs
black against the light, thirty years
ago, and the good girl—what's her name—
believing, or think about the dog
he beat to death that day in Carbonado?

I hear he's dead, and wait now on my porch.
He must be in his shack. The wagon's
due to come and take him where they take
late alcoholics, probably called Farm's End.
I plan my frown, certain he'll be carried out
bleeding from the corners of his grin.

Duwamish

Midwestern in the heat, this river's
curves are slow and sick. Water knocks
at mills and concrete plants, and crud
compounds the gray. On the out-tide,
water, half salt water from the sea,
rambles by a barrel of molded nails,
gray lumber piles, moss on ovens
in the brickyard no one owns.
Boys are snapping tom cod spines
and jeering at the Greek who bribes
the river with his sailing coins.

Because the name is Indian, Indians
ignore the river as it cruises
past the tavern. Gulls are diving crazy
where boys nail porgies to the pile.
No Indian would interrupt his beer
to tell the story of the snipe
who dove to steal the nailed girl
late one autumn, with the final salmon in.

This river colors day. On bright days
here, the sun is always setting or obscured
by one cloud. Or the shade extended
to the far bank just before you came.
And what should flare, the Chinese red
of a searun's-fin, the futile roses,

unkept cherry trees in spring, is muted.
For the river, there is late November
only, and the color of a slow winter.

On the short days, looking for a word,
knowing the smoke from the small homes
turns me colder than wind from
the cold river, knowing this poverty
is not a lack of money but of friends,
I come here to be cold. Not silver cold
like ice, for ice has glitter. Gray
cold like the river. Cold like 4 P.M.
on Sunday. Cold like a decaying porgy.

But cold is a word. There is no word along
this river I can understand or say.
Not Greek threats to a fishless moon
nor Slavic chants. All words are Indian.
Love is Indian for water, and madness
means, to Redmen, I am going home.

The Way a Ghost Behaves

Knock or none, that woman hears a knocking,
runs to the door, ready for a friend—
only frost in moonlight and the dog
she cannot stand.

She believes that God is in the trees,
perched like a bird, waiting for the crumbs
she scatters on
the snow for definite robins.

Love to her is mystery and pain.
Her children died
and winter puts a creaking in the house
that makes her sing and grin.

Her garden works
because, early on the first warm day
while others wait the official end of winter
her hoe is ringing rocks away.

Deaf or not, that woman hears me knocking,
runs to the door, ready for a friend—
only rain and darkness and a man
she'd love again.

No Bells to Believe

When bells ring, wild rain pelts the river.
Who rings bells in the abandoned chapel,
once a school, once a shed where hide
was stored? The painter painting reeds
a private color, poppy farmer,
and the seiner folding autumn's nets—
they hear the bells and don't look up.

Mad Sam, the nutty preacher rings the bells.
He remained despite that mess, twelve
years back—the squaw—the poisoned wine.
Not Sam. He drowned beneath a boom.

No bells. Even when Mad Sam went mad
with God each Sunday and the women wept
to hear their imperfections yelled across
the river while a drum knocked Jesus
senseless and the tugboats tooted home.
No bells then. None now. What rings here
is something in the air unnamed.

The wild rain rings. The painter's reeds
run down the canvas in a colorful
defeat, the seiner's nets gain weight
and poppies wash away. The women told
Mad Sam before he ran out on the logs,
you must accept the ringing like the day.

At the Stilli's Mouth

This river ground to quiet in Sylvana.
Here, the quick birds limp and age
or in flight run out of breath and quit.
Poplars start and then repeat the wind
and wind repeats the dust that cakes the girl
who plays a game of wedding in the road
where cars have never been. The first car
will be red and loaded with wild grooms.

August rain says go to blackmouth,
violate the tin piled derelict against
the barn and glowing like the luck
a fugitive believed until he found
this land too flat for secrets
and the last hill diving on him
like a starved bird. The crude dike,
slag and mud and bending out of sight,
left gray the only color for the sky,
wind the only weather, neo-Holland
printed with no laughter on the map.

That hermit in the trailer at the field's
forgotten corner, he has moments, too—
a perfect solo on a horn he cannot play,
applauding sea, special gifts of violets
and cream. In bed at 5 P.M.
he hears the rocks of children on his roof
threatening his right to waste his life.

21

With the Stilli this defeated and the sea
turned slough by close Camano, how can water die
with drama, in a final rich cascade,
a suicide, a victim of terrain, a martyr?
Or need it die? Can't the stale sea tunnel,
climb and start the stream again
somewhere in the mountains where the clinks
of trickle on the stones remind the fry
ending is where rain and blackmouth runs begin?

Now the blackmouth run. The Stilli quivers
where it never moved before. Willows
change to windmills in the spiteless eye.
Listen. Fins are cracking like the wings
of quick birds trailing rivers through the sky.

The Way a Ghost Dissolves

Where she lived the close remained the best.
The nearest music and the static cloud,
sun and dirt were all she understood.
She planted corn and left the rest
to elements, convinced that God
with giant faucets regulates the rain
and saves the crops from frost or foreign wind.

Fate assisted her with special cures.
Rub a half potato on your wart
and wrap it in a damp cloth. Close
your eyes and whirl three times and throw.
Then bury rag and spud exactly where
they fall. The only warts that I have now
are memories or comic on my nose.

Up at dawn. The earth provided food
if worked and watered, planted green
with rye grass every fall. Or driven wild
by snakes that kept the carrots clean,
she butchered snakes and carrots with a hoe.
Her screams were sea birds in the wind,
her chopping—nothing like it now.

I will garden on the double run,
my rhythm obvious in ringing rakes,
and trust in fate to keep me poor and kind
and work until my heart is short,

then go out slowly with a feeble grin,
my fingers flexing but my eyes gone gray
from cramps and the lack of oxygen.

Forget the tone. Call the neighbor's trumpet
golden as it grates. Exalt the weeds.
Say the local animals have class
or help me say that ghost has gone to seed.
And why attempt to see the cloud again—
the screaming face it was before it cracked
in wind from Asia and a wanton rain.

from *Death of the Kapowsin Tavern* (1965)

Introduction to the Hoh

Nearly all the rivers color like the sky
and bend in other places after extra pour.
This blueness is high ice. Cartographers
are smiling at the curves that will recur.

See the white in spring, the milk flow
high enough to run the smaller aspens down.
See there is no urge to lay the sun
across your going like a greasewood patch.

Think of stark abundance, a famous run of jacks
the vanished tribe at the mouth once bragged about.
Think of hungry Mays, the nets reversed
to snag what rot the river washes out.

Glacial melt and tinge are slight in autumn.
Cutthroat backs and pools retain the blue.
Remember famine as these broken leaves
ride away like Indians from you.

Between the Bridges

These shacks are tricks. A simple smoke
from wood stoves, hanging half-afraid
to rise, makes poverty in winter real.
Behind unpainted doors, old Greeks
are counting money with their arms.
Different birds collect for crumbs
each winter. The loners don't
but ought to wear red shawls.

Here, a cracked brown hump
of knuckle caved a robber's skull.
That cut fruit is for Slavic booze.
Jars of fruit-spiked bourbon bake
on roofs throughout July; festive tubs
of vegetables get wiser in the sun.
All men are strong. Each woman knows
how river cod can be preserved.

Money is for life. Let the money
pile up thirty years and more.
Not in banks, but here, in shacks
where green is real: the stacks of tens
and twenties and the moss on broken piles
big ships tied to when the river
and the birds ran painted to the sea.

Plunking the Skagit

It's mystery, not wind, the men
endure. Steelhead drew them here
where tons of winter drive above
them north and fires start the day
along the bar. A hundred feet
of nylon settles on the river
and the wait begins. Each line slants
tight from an upright rod to water
and underwater to the pencil lead.
A flat south: wind will hammer
water from their eyes, wind and water motion
faking knocks of steelhead in the bells.

These men are never cold. Their faces
burn with winter and their eyes
are hot. They see, across the flat,
the black day coming for them
and the black sea. Good wind
mixes with the bourbon in their bones.

A real name—steelhead—rainbow
from the sea. He runs in summer, too
but that is undramatic, the river
down and warm. No pour to push against.
No ice to snap his fins. No snow
to lay him on for photographs.

Men keep warm with games. The steelhead
is a Burmese spy, a hired gun
from Crete. He comes to mate, not die
on some forgotten sand like salmon.
He rides the river out in spring
planning then his drive for next
December, when big rains bring him
roaring from the sea with fins on fire.

This near the mouth, the river barely glides.
One man thinks the birds that nick
the river mark the fish. Birds believe
the men are evergreens. Above
the guess and ruffle, in the wind—
steelhead to the spawning ground.

Hideout

In the reeds, the search for food by grebes
is brief. Each day, inside the shack
the wind paints white, a man keeps warm
by listening to ships go by, keeps sane
by counting European faces
passing north in clouds. Tugs deposit
miles of logs outside. A tax collector
couldn't find this place with holy maps.

When salmon crowd each other
in the river, and the river boils
with re-creation's anger, what tall man
re-creates too clearly domes of mills
downstream, and the gradual opening
as if the river loved the city
or was crying loudly "take me" to the sea?
What odd games children play.
One shouts himself into a president.
Another pins the villain salmon
to the air with spears. A rowboat
knocks all night against a pile.

Morning brings a new wind and a new
white coat of weather for the shack.
The salmon moved upstream last night
and no bird cuts the river, looking
for a smelt. Ships sail off to Naples
and the bent face bobbing in the wake
was counted in another cloud gone north.

Duwamish Head

1.

That girl upstream was diced by scaling knives—
scattered in the shack I licked her knees in
where she tossed me meat and called me dog
and I would dive a dog at her from stars,
wind around my ears—violins and shot.

With salmon gone and industry moved in
birds don't bite the water. Once this river
brought a cascade color to the sea.
Now the clouds are cod, crossing on the prowl
beneath the dredge that heaps a hundred tons
of crud on barges for the dumping ground.

My vision started at this river mouth,
on a slack tide, trying to catch bullheads
in a hopeless mud. The pier was caving
from the weight of gulls. Wail of tug
and trawl, a town not growing up
across the bay, rotten pay for kings—
these went by me like the secret dawns
the sea brought in. I saw the seaperch
turn and briefly flare around a pile
and disappear. I heard bent men
beg a sole to look less like a stone.

Beyond the squatters and the better homes
stars were good to dive from. Scattered

in the shack I licked her knees in.
Diced, the paper said, by scaling knives.

2.

River, I have loved, loved badly on your bank.
On your out-tide drain I ride toward the sea
so deep the blue cries out in pain from weight.
Loved badly you and years of misery
in shacks along your bank—cruel women
and their nervous children—fishhooks filed
for easy penetration—cod with cracked necks
reaching with their gills for one more day.
Last year's birds are scouting for the kill,
hysterical as always when the smelt run thin.

Jacks don't run. Mills go on polluting
and the river hot with sewage steams.
In bourbon sleep, old men hummed salmon
home to mountains and the river jammed
with blackmouth, boiled in moonlight while the mills
boomed honest sparks. October rolled
with dorsal fins and no man ruled the runs.

When I see a stream, I like to say: exactly.
Where else could it run? Trace it back to ice.
Try to find a photo of your cradle.
Rivers jump their beds and don't look back
regretting they have lost such lovely rides.

I could name those birds, see people
in the clouds. Sight can be polluted
like a river. When this river asks me:
where were you when Slavs gave up their names
to find good homes on paved streets west of here?
I talk back. What are you, river?
Only water, taking any bed you find.

All you have is current, doubled back
on in-tide, screaming out on out.
I am on your bank, blinded and alive.

3.
Where cod and boys had war, a bolt plant roars.
Sparks are stars. Next Sunday, when I die
no drunk will groan my name in spasms
as he vomits last night from the dock.
I have memories of heat upstream.
Her arms and eyes had power like the river
and she imitated salmon with a naked roll.

My vision started at this river mouth
and stuck here (bullhead in the mud)
a third of what could be a lifetime.
The city blares and fishermen are rich.
Tugs and trawls repainted slide to ports
and perch found better color in the sea.

My fins are hands. The river, once
so verbal drifts with such indifference
by me I am forced to shout my name:
backing up on in-tide, screaming out on out—
river, I have loved, loved badly on your bank.

Scattered in the shack I licked her knees in—
beyond her, nothing, just the Indian
I use so often infantile in dreams
of easy winters, five-day runs of silvers,
festive bakes, the passing of the jacks
to sand pools promised by the rain.

To know is to be alien to rivers.
This river helped me play an easy role—
to be alone, to drink, to fail.

The world goes on with money. A tough cat
dove here from a shingle mill on meat
that glittered as it swam. The mill is gone.
The cat is ground. If I say love
was here, along the river, show me bones
of cod, scales and blood, faces in the clouds
so thick they jam the sky with laughter.

Tahola

Where sea breaks inland, claiming the Quinalt
in a half saltwater lake, canoes turn gray
waiting for the runs. The store makes money
but the two cafés, not open, rot in spray.
Baskets you can buy are rumored Cherokee.
When kings run wild, girls use salmon oil
to stain a doll's face real. The best house
was never envied for its tile. Cars
and philosophic eyes are coated by the sea.

Whites pay well to motor up the river,
harvest blackmouth, humpbacks, silvers,
jacks and sea run cuts. Where rain assaults
the virgin timber and the fishpools boil,
the whites pry stories from the guide
with bourbon. Sunset, and they putt downriver
singing. But the wind, the sea
make all music language, dead as a wet drum.

When whites drive off and the money's gone
a hundred mongrels bark. Indians
should mend the tribal nets in moonlight,
not drink more and hum a white man's tune
they heard upstream. What about the words?
Something about war, translated by the sea
and wind into a song a doll sang
long ago, riding a crude wave in.

Road Ends at Tahola

My nostrils tell me: somewhere *mare nostro*.
Here the wolf-fish hides his lumpy face in shame.
Pines lean east and groan. Odors of a booze
that's contraband, are smuggled in by storms.
Our booze is legal Irish and our eyes
develop felons in the endless spray.
Mare nostro somewhere, and eternity's
a law, not a felony like here.
That derelict was left for storms to break.

One ship passes denting the horizon,
creeping down the world. Whatever gave us pride
(food en route to Rio) dies. The wake could be
that wave we outrun laughing up the sand.
Night comes on with stars and years of dead fish
lighting foam with phosphorus they left.
All day the boom was protest, sea against
the moon. *Mare nostro* somewhere and no shame.

Remember once, a scene, a woman naked
clowning in the sea while armies laughed.
Her man, a clown, had courage and he came
and hauled her (both were sobbing) up the stones.
If I were strong, if wolf-fish didn't dive
beyond the range of scorn, you'd be alive.

I can't say *mare nostro*. Groaning pines
won't harm you, leaning east on galaxies.

I know I'm stone. My voice is ugly.
A kelp bed is a rotten place to hide.
Listen. Hear the booming. See the gleam,
the stars that once were fish and died.
We kiss between the fire and the ocean.
In the morning we will start another stare
across the gray. Nowhere *mare nostro*.
Don't claim it and the sea belongs to you.

Eileen

Why this day you're going so much wind?
When you've gone I'll go back in alone
and take the stillest corner in the house—
the dark one where your dark-eyed ghost
will find me whipped and choking back my rage.
I won't show my hatred to their food.
I have to live here with these shaking hands.

Find a home with heat, some stranger
who's indifferent to your dirty dress
and loves you for that quiet frown
you'll own until you die or kiss.
The wind is drowning out the car
and raising dust so you can disappear
the way you used to playing in the fern.

Some day I'll be too big for them to hit,
too fast to catch, too quick to face the cross
and go away by fantasy or mule
and take revenge on matrons for your loss
and mail you word of faces I have cut.
Be patient when the teasers call you fat.
I'll join you later for a wordless meal.

Then I'll stroke the maggots from your hair.
They come for me now you're not here.
I wax their statues, croak out hymns
they want and wait for dust to settle

on the road you left on centuries ago,
believing you were waving, knowing
it was just a bird who crossed the road
behind you and the sunlight off the car.

What the Brand New Freeway Won't Go By

The block is bare except for this five-story
ugly brick hotel. Perhaps the bulk
frightened stores and homes away. Age is clear
in turrets and the milk on window sills.
The new name and the outside coat of paint
must have raised the rent. As you drive by
the rooms seem yellow and the air inside
is stale because a roomer, second floor,
in underwear, unshaven, fries a meal.

To live here you should be a friend of rain,
and fifty with a bad job on the freights,
knowing the freeway soon will siphon
the remaining world away
and you can die unseen among your photos—
swimmers laughing but the day remembered cold.

Rooms have gas. The place was in the papers.
Police have issued statements about cancer
and the case is closed, but not the jokes
passing boys are drilling through the walls.
Top-floor renters look down floors of sweat
to traffic that might stop were they to go.
Some rooms are paid for in advance with shock.

If, when the freeway opens, a man
afraid of speed still takes this road,

the faded Under New Management sign
might mean to him: we are older too—
live here—we'll never treat you badly again.

December 24 and George McBride Is Dead

You a gentleman and I up from the grime—
now wind has shut your dark, dark eyes
and I am left to hate this Christmas eve.
Christ, they're playing carols. Some crap
never stops. You're dead and I'm without
one goddam Wagner record in the house
to play you up to what for some must be
behind the sky with solid orchestration.

Rest in your defeat, you stupid jerk,
so fat your heart gave out, so sweet
you couldn't help but hear the punks.
"One gulp. The whole quart, Mac." That town
you died in—so unlikely—vineyards,
sunny valleys, stark white missions
and the pale priest summoning
brown sinners from the olive grove.
I'll not know your grave, though I believe
our minds have music that can lead us
through the tangle to the lost stone of a friend.

I get along, write my poems. Essentially
a phony, I try my feelings now
and know I fail. George, it's Christmas eve
and bells are caroling. I'm in the kitchen,
fat and writing, drinking beer and shaking.

Port Townsend

On cliffs above the town, high homes disdain
what is not Victorian below
but Indian or cruel. A plaque declares
a chapel older than the town.
(Many worship God before they're born.)
The Keystone ferry sails without a car,
a passenger, not even trailing gulls.
The pulp mill shoots bad odor at the sun.

Arriving here is feeling some old love—
half a memory—a silly dream of how
a war would end, a world would settle down
with time for hair to gray before you die.
The other half of memory is sight.
The cliffs will hold another thousand years.
The town is rotting every Sunday night.

A novel fakes a start in every bar,
gives way to gin and talk. The talk gives way
to memories of elk, and elk were never here.
Freighters never give this town a second look.
The dead are buried as an afterthought
and when the tide comes glittering with smelt
the grebes have gone to look for meaty ports.

Fort Casey, Without Guns

The iron doors we shut on ammo rooms
slam like a heart attack. Had the guns remained,
grass would still be busted by July to straw
and riptides groan as current doubles back
in hatred. Concrete walls were hopes
of pioneers, one shade deeper gray each spring.
From these emplacements, ten-inch cannons tracked
fifty years of freighters down the strait.
The sea shot out the gunners' eyes with light.
The army moved to Coupeville in defeat.

What's left to save, the riptide will protect.
We joke our way through battlements,
dim powder huts, the corridors where words explode
and we are skeletons, trapped by a mistake—
the wrong door closed, a turn we didn't make.
We claw at rungs to take us into sky.

Straw bales on the muster ground deny
a need for war. The farmer doesn't care.
The strait can go unguarded, pagan ships
sail in with slave girls and a threat of fun—
the Stars-and-Stripes torn down—the Constitution
used to start a fire for the wienie roast.
Only harvest matters. Here, the army
harvested no enemy. Even boredom cracked—
contraband steamed down in 'twenty-eight—
the bootleg wink—rum for rotting men.

Best to come here when the picnics peter out.
On dark days, gulls are shells (man will not disarm)
and we can play our war. I am a captain.
Make that cloud salute. The Olympics
bomb the strait with shadow. In the meadow
where October green begins, cattle eat
and children point their space guns at us,
crying boom the booming sea can't hear.

The Church on Comiaken Hill

The lines are keen against today's bad sky
about to rain. We're white and understand
why Indians sold butter for the funds
to build this church. Four hens and a rooster
huddle on the porch. We are dark
and know why no one climbed to pray. The priest
who did his best to imitate a bell
watched the river, full of spirits, coil
below the hill, relentless for the bay.

A church abandoned to the wind is portent.
In high wind, ruins make harsh music.
The priest is tending bar. His dreams have paid
outrageous fees for stone and mortar.
His eyes are empty as a chapel
roofless in a storm. Greek temples seem
the same as forty centuries ago.
If we used one corner for a urinal,
he wouldn't swear we hadn't worshipped here.

The chickens cringe. Rain sprays chaos where
the altar and the stained glass would have gone
had Indians not eaten tribal cows
one hungry fall. Despite the chant,
salmon hadn't come. The first mass
and a phone line cursed the river.
If rain had rhythm, it would not be Latin.

Children do not wave as we drive out.
Like these graves ours may go unmarked.
Can we be satisfied when dead
with daffodils for stones? These Indians—
whatever they once loved or used for God—
the hill—the river—the bay burned by the moon—
they knew that when you die you lose your name.

The Blond Road

This road dips and climbs but never bends.
The line it finally is strings far beyond
my sight, still the color of useless dirt.
Trees are a hundred greens in varying light
as sky breaks black on silver over and in
the sea. Not one home or car. No shacks
abandoned to the storms. On one side,
miles of high grass; on the other, weather
and the sea reflecting tons of a wild day.

The wind is from Malay. Tigers in the wind
make lovers claw each other orange. Blond
dirt rises to recite the lies of summer
before the wind goes north and cats rip
white holes in the sky. Fields are grim
and birds along this road are always stone.

I planned to cheat the road with laughter.
Build a home no storm could crack
and sing my Fridays over centuries of water—
once more, have me back, my awkward weather—
but the land is not for sale. Centuries
are strung: a blond road north and south
and no man will improve it with macadam.

The road is greased by wind. Sun has turned
the blond dirt brown, the brown grass
black and dark ideas of the ocean

silver. Each month rolls along the road
with an hour's effort. Now the lovers
can't recall each other or identify
that roar: the northern pain of tigers.

I know that just a word I'll never have
could make the brown road blond again
and send the stone birds climbing to their names.

Death of the Kapowsin Tavern

I can't ridge it back again from char.
Not one board left. Only ash a cat explores
and shattered glass smoked black and strung
about from the explosion I believe
in the reports. The white school up for sale
for years, most homes abandoned to the rocks
of passing boys—the fire, helped by wind
that blew the neon out six years before,
simply ended lots of ending.

A damn shame. Now, when the night chill
of the lake gets in a troller's bones
where can the troller go for bad wine
washed down frantically with beer?
And when wise men are in style again
will one recount the two-mile glide of cranes
from dead pines or the nameless yellow
flowers thriving in the useless logs,
or dots of light all night about the far end
of the lake, the dawn arrival of the idiot
with catfish—most of all, above the lake
the temple and our sanctuary there?

Nothing dies as slowly as a scene.
The dusty jukebox cracking through
the cackle of a beered-up crone—
wagered wine—sudden need to dance—

these remain in the black debris.
Although I know in time the lake will send
wind black enough to blow it all away.

from *Good Luck in Cracked Italian* (1969)

Docking at Palermo

You can't weep like them, can't pound the rail
with love for this or any land.
You never understood a cloudy north
so how these tears or that syllabic sun?
This rock that came at you for hours
came at others twenty years ago
in dread. You pass the bay
where they invaded, saying it was wrong.
On either side a cliff and raining guns.

The dolphins had their fling and now
Palermo comes. Blue dots on your right
are welders welding ships. Other dots
are neon just turned on, others
faces strained from waiting on the dock
and now the son is old and home to die.
If you went home a bear would turn away.

For them, the gangplank's down. For you
a cheating cabby waits. Learn the names
of streets or give them names to fight.
You have five hours here. If here before
with hate, you walk a street called war
and beg a man who was a beggar then:
now I have no gun, show me how to cry.

Napoli Again

Long before I hear it, Naples bright
with buildings trumpets from the hill.
A tugboat toots *"paisan"* and I am back.
That dock I sailed from eighteen years ago.
This bay had a fleet of half-sunk ships.
Where those dapper men are drinking wine,
a soldier beat an urchin with a belt.
Fountains didn't work. I remember stink.
Streets and buildings all seemed brown.

Romans hate such recent ruins,
bombed-out houses you do not repair.
Better pillars one must work to date.
Forget the innocent cut down,
cats gone crazy from the bombs
waiting down those alleys for delicious eyes.
Here, the glass replaced in *galleria* roofs,
cappuccino too high priced, it's hard
to go back years and feed the whores for free.

I'll never think of virgin angels here.
Did I walk this street before,
protesting: I am kind. You switch the menu,
gyp me on the bill. Remember me? My wings?
The silver target and the silver bomb?
Take the extra coin. I only came
to see you living and the fountains run.

Galileo's Chair

In gold light here a small guard
warns me not to cross the velvet chain
or climb the stairs that might break down
beneath my modern bulk. Galileo's telescope
was not the first but first toward
the sky. The milky way's not milk
and Venus circles in and out of light.

Take air away and even fire falls—
a voice through this tan air, across
these tiers, seducing men to think.
Star without parallax, he measured time
by weight, like men, and moons of Jupiter
were cause for wine. Sagredo warned
of Roman hate so heavy it can crack
the latest lens. No Pope honors proof
we move about the sun. God is weight
enough to bend an unrecanting knee.

He may be wrong. The sun may circle men.
The stairs might hold me but his chair,
inelegant and worn, is the odd star
fixed beyond my chain. The brown wood
turns this hall a darker brown
each year. We'll give in too and air
will darken in Peking. Outside, pigeons
called by bells of Padova
to fan about a tower, highest point

for miles, the first and last to catch
the sun, won't fly or will fly blind.

I never cross the chain. The small guard
tries to talk but my Italian's stuck.
Was the dungeon black? The one he went to
when he'd lied to God, and where he said
eppur si muove and it did.

Kennedy Ucciso

Don't scream at me you God damn' wops,
nine at night. I know what the headline says.
Blasted by some creep in Dallas.
Don't ask me who Johnson is.
Don't ask *racismo, comunismo?*
I don't know. That fountain lit
and flowing over naked ladies, fish,
animals and birds, is blurred. You and words
in giant print keep banging at my head.

I voted for him, not my kind of man.
My kind could not be president,
just a target for the cold. You slip in
noisy knives of why. *Un gran uomo?*
Certamente. I know, here this very year.
Yes, a Catholic. Yes. Yes. Very rich.
A man who put some sixty million lives
on some vague line and won.
I'd vote for him again. But here
in the *piazza* where the fountain
makes wet love to ladies and stone swans
I want your questions and my hate to end.

The fountain runs in thighs of lovely stone.
Ladies do quite well, subduing swans
and lizards, giving in to fish. You Romans,
quite *simpatici.* Someday we'll be you.
I weep in the *piazza*, perfect wop.

Take your questions to a sainted star.
My Italian fails. *Come si dice:*
He was not afraid of what we are.

April in Cerignola

This is Puglia and cruel. The sun is mean
all summer and the *tramontana*
whips the feeble four months into March.
It was far too tense. Off the streets by five.
Flyers screaming begging children off
and flyers stabbed. The only beauty
is the iron grillwork, and neither that
nor spring was here when I was young.

It used to be my town. The closest one
for bomb-bomb boys to buy *spumanti* in.
It reeked like all the towns. Italian men
were gone. The women locked themselves in dark
behind the walls, the bullet holes patched now.
Dogs could sense the madness and went mute.
The streets were mute despite the cry
of children: give me cigarette. But always flat—
the land in all directions and the time.

I was desolate, too, and so survived.
I had a secret wish, to bring much food
and feed you through the war. I wished
you also dead. All roads lead to none.
You're too far from the Adriatic
to get good wind. Harsh heat and roaring cold
are built in like abandonment each year.
And every day, these mean streets open
knowing there's no money and no fun.

So why return? You tell me I'm the only one
came back, and you're amazed
I haven't seen Milan. I came in August
and went home in March, with no chance
to experience the miles of tall grain
jittering in wind, and olive trees
alive from recent rain. You're still my town.
The men returned. The women opened doors.
The hungry lived and grew, had children
they can feed. Most of all, the streets are wide,
lead nowhere, and dying in your weather
takes a lifetime of surviving last year's war.

Spinazzola: Quella Cantina Là

A field of wind gave license for defeat.
I can't explain. The grass bent. The wind
seemed full of men but without hate or fame.
I was farther than that farm where the road
slants off to nowhere, and the field I'm sure
is in this wine or that man's voice. The man
and this canteen were also here
twenty years ago and just as old.

Hate for me was dirt until I woke up
five miles over Villach in a smoke
that shook my tongue. Here, by accident,
the wrong truck, I came back to the world.
This canteen is home-old. A man can walk
the road outside without a song or gun.
I can't explain the wind. The field is east
toward the Adriatic from my wine.

I'd walked from cruel soil to a trout
for love but never from a bad sky
to a field of wind I can't explain.
The drone of bombers going home
made the weather warm. My uniform
turned foreign where the olive trees
throw silver to each other down the hill.

Olive leaves were silver I could spend.
Say wind I can't explain. That field is vital

and the Adriatic warm. Don't our real friends
tell us when we fail? Don't honest fields
reveal us in their winds? Planes and men
once tumbled but the war went on absurd.
I can't explain the wine. This crude bench
and rough table and that flaking plaster—
most of all the long nights make this home.

Home's always been a long way from a friend.
I mix up things, the town, the wind, the war.
I can't explain the drone. Bombers seemed
to scream toward the target, on the let-down
hum. My memory is weak from bombs.
Say I dropped them bad with shaking sight.
Call me German and my enemy the air.

Clouds are definite types. High ones, cirrus.
Cumulus, big fluffy kind, and if with rain,
also nimbus. Don't fly into them.
I can't explain. Somewhere in a gray ball
wind is killing. I forgot the stratus
high and thin. I forget my field
of wind, out there east between
the Adriatic and my second glass of wine.

I'll find the field. I'll go feeble down
the road strung gray like spoiled wine
in the sky. A sky too clear of cloud
is fatal. Trust the nimbus. Trust dark clouds
to rain. I can't explain the sun. The man
will serve me wine until a bomber fleet
lost twenty years comes droning home.

I can't explain. Outside, on the road
that leaves the town reluctantly,
way out the road's a field of wind.

Galleria Umberto I

Now it's clean. The whores seem healthy
and the bombed-out panes have been replaced.
This arcade's a monument to money,
in a city with a desperate need
for money, in a country with no need at all
for love. These shops will never sell
those gaudy chandeliers. The gaudy whores
display themselves forever with no takers.

I remember it a little more forlorn.
Not just roof glass gone, but harsh arrays
of junk on tables and pathetic faces
crying for ten lire. There were faces
broken by the war, and faces warped
by cruelty they'd learned, and faces gone.
I kept my face by turning it away.
It was here that John Horne Burns
saw war summed up, the cracked life
going on, taking what it would in gesture
and a beggar's bitter hand.

There's no metaphor for pain, despair.
It's just there. You live with it, if lucky
in a poem, or try to see it, how it was
under this dome roof with children dead,
the stench of death blown at you
off a sea we should have asked for wisdom
by wind we still should beg for tears.

In all our years, we come to only this:
capacity to harm, to starve, to claim
I'm not myself. I didn't do these things.

I did lots of things and I'm myself
to live with, bad as any German.
It's a place to start undoing. The whore
is certain in a storm that when it dies
new ships come in. How could this poem
with no tough man behind it, come to me
today, walking where I walked
twenty years ago amazed, when now
no one is hungry, the gold facade is polished
and they have no word in dialect for lonely?

Maratea Porto

In winter, Germans gone, the sea insane
explodes for miles and stutters, foam birds
down the stone. Back home, we prayed for this,
a cobbled street, the sand swept clean by storm,
always weather at us, lightning, sun,
and out there Sicily unseen, or rain
en route to where we stand, beside the ruin,
Saracen, where lookouts looked and waited
for the glint of a devoted mob.

The mongoloid cast out by family to beg,
the epileptic throwing seizures in the road,
church bells that won't let you think,
rats and fleas, the cats who scrounge for food—
all unforeseen. Back home we hide what's wrong.
The gong is soft except when rung for meals.
Here, far more than lovely lava caves
the sea gouged out, much more than crosses
on the mountain tops, the hands of women
cut by grass they pull and rope they weave
from grass, the hands and minds of man
gone stone from stone and sweat and little pay
are what we see and what we must believe.

And here we must believe the bombing spray,
the sea attenuated by the stone, squeezed in
until it screams relief and rockets to the moon

ahead of man. But also man, that Saracen who stares forever in the boiling wind beside his ruin, waiting for his day.

Cantina Iannini

Walls were painted blue so long ago, you think
of old sky you thought lovely turned as it did,
in your lifetime, dirty. Six crude wood tables
and the pregnant cat seem permanent
on the pockmarked concrete floor. The owner
gives too much away, too much free wine
and from his eyes too much grief. His facial lines
amplify in light the two small windows
and the opaque door glass flatten out.
To enter you should be poor by consent.

You and the world that hurts you should agree
you don't deserve a penny. Nor a clear tongue
to beg sympathy from wine dark as your life
and rich as your dream you still are nothing in.
And you should agree to cross your throat
and weep when the casket passes. You should kneel
when wind crosses the olive grove in waves
of stuttering coin. At nine the light goes down.
You weave home to homes you'll never own.

Only men in broken rags come back
to drink black wine under the painting
Moonlight on Sea a drunk thought lovely—
turned as it did, in his liftime, muddy.
You hear the wind outside turn white. Wasn't
some loud promise in another wine? Sea cliff
with a girl, her hair streamed out your lifetime

down the sky? Your wine is dead. Tomorrow
you'll return to this grim charm, not quite broken,
not quite ready to release your eyes.

Maratea Porto: The Dear Postmistress There

I run up the stairs too fast every morning
and panting for mail, I stagger inside
and there she sits wagging a negative finger.
Her frown is etched in and her mouth is sour.
Niente per voi, today.

This is Odysseus. I've come a long way.
I've beaten a giant, real mean with one eye.
Even the sea. I've defeated the water.
But now I'm home, pooped. Where's Penelope?
Niente per voi, today.

My name is Joseph and this, my wife Mary.
we've had a long journey and Mary is heavy.
The facts are odd. The child could be holy
and I wonder, have you a room in your inn?
Niente per voi, today.

I'm Genghis Khan and this is my army.
We've conquered your land. Now we want women.
Bring them today at high noon to the square.
After we've had them, we'll get out of here.
Niente per voi, today.

I'm Michelangelo, here to make statues.
I've lugged this damn marble all the way from the Alps.
I'll need a large scaffold and plenty of ropes,

a chisel, a mallet and oodles of wine.
Niente per voi, today.

Oh, heroes of time, you're never a hero
until you've endured ten days with no mail.
Slaughter the stars and come home in splendor.
She'll always be there at the end of the trail.
Niente per voi, today.

South Italy, Remote and Stone

The enemy's not poverty. It's wind.
Morning it beats you awake to the need
for hoeing and hoeing rock. The priest proclaims
it's not a futile wind. This air moves
with undercurrents of hope five stunted
olive trees pick up. You live all year
on the gallon of olives you sell
and hope the stone will be soil
enough to grow something in. Your hoe and wind
have fought this stone forever and lost.

Up north, the kind have issued your name:
paese abbandonato. It rings now
in this wind that clears my eyes. Your hands
are not abandoned, and the harsh length
of each day forces you to love whatever is—
a screaming wife, a child who has stared
from birth. The road I came on must be old
or some state accident. In heat, this place
is African. In cold, a second moon.

Even your tongue is hard. Syllables whip
and demons, always deposited cruel
in the prettiest unmarried girl,
must be whipped by the priest into air
where bells can drive them to rivers. Or she
will be sent out forever, alone on the roads
with her madness, no chance to be saved

by a prince or kind ox. And so on, a test
of your love. Only the ugly survive.

I'm still alive. My love was tested and passed
something like this. Much better soil.
A more favorable chance at the world.
I sent myself out forever on roads.
I'll never be home except here, dirt poor
in abandoned country. My enemy, wind,
helps me hack each morning again at the rock.

Remote Farm on the Dubrovnik-Sarajevo Run

Each afternoon the world goes by above it
on the train. Maybe I look down with envy
on the thin strip, the only flat spot
in this jagged land. The strip was cleared
of stone so long ago the stony hill that falls
long and steep toward it from the train, the gulch
that falls off on the other side, seem younger
than the farm. They plant their dead between
the house and where the brown men plow.

All so certain. Where you're born, you die.
That first of many terrifying days, a child
can stare his plot into a whale, or stare until
he knows exactly how his grave dug out
will look, a rich cut into soil
nothing grows in now. He must know he'll endure
the quakes, the shifting snow, the rain
that flashes down the boulders every spring
to sweep the farmland clean, to ready land
for planting. He must know other children
will respect his name because Cyrillic
settles like the weather into stone.

From tyranny the road out goes to states
more frightening than rage. If you run away
you cut your feet, your first scream comes back
doubled in the city, and one day old walls
seem like arms. I'll stay on the train

to Sarajevo, remembering a graveyard
in the country, a hot day and a woman
with a blue bouquet asking me directions
to a stone someone way back forgot to mark.

Montesano Unvisited

With houses hung that slanted and remote
the road that goes there if you found it
would be dangerous and dirt. Dust would cake
the ox you drive by and you couldn't meet
the peasant stare that drills you black. Birds
might be at home but rain would feel rejected
in the rapid drain and wind would bank off
fast without a friend to stars. Inside
the convent they must really mean those prayers.

You never find the road. You pass the cemetery,
military, British, World War Two and huge.
Maybe your car will die and the garage
you go to will be out of parts. The hotel
you have to stay in may have postcard shots,
deep focus stuff, of graves close up
and far off, just as clear, the bright town
that is someone's grave. Towns are bad things happening,
a spear elected mayor, a whip ordained.
You know in that town there's a beautiful girl
you'd rescue if your horse could run.

When your car is fixed you head on north
sticking with the highway, telling yourself
if you'd gone it would have been no fun.
Mountain towns are lovely, hung way away
like that, throbbing in light. But stay in one
two hours. You pat your car and say

let's go, friend. You drive off never hearing
the bruised girl in the convent screaming
take me with you. I am not a nun.

from *The Lady in*
Kicking Horse Reservoir (1973)

A Map of Montana in Italy

On this map white. A state thick as a fist
or blunt instrument. Long roads weave and cross
red veins full of rage. Big Canada, map maker's
pink, squats on our backs, planning bad winters
for years, and Glacier Park's green with my envy
of Grizzly Bears. On the right, antelope sail
between strands of barbed wire and never
get hurt, west, I think, of Plevna, say near
Sumatra, or more west, say Shawmut,
anyway, on the right, east on the plains.
The two biggest towns are dull deposits
of men getting along, making money, driving
to church every Sunday, censoring movies and books.
The two most interesting towns, Helena, Butte,
have the good sense to fail. There's too much
schoolboy in bars—I'm tougher than you—
and too much talk about money.
Jails and police are how you dream Poland—
odd charges, bad food and forms you must fill
stating your religion. In Poland say none.
With so few Negroes and Jews we've been reduced
to hating each other, dumping our crud
in our rivers, mistreating the Indians.
Each year, 4000 move, most to the west
where ocean currents keep winter in check.
This map is white, meaning winter, ice
where you are, helping children who may be
already frozen. It's white here too

but back of me, up in the mountains where
the most ferocious animals
are obsequious wolves. No one fights
in the bars filled with pastry. There's no
prison for miles. But last night the Italians
cheered the violence in one of our westerns.

The Milltown Union Bar

(*Laundromat & Cafe*)
You could love here, not the lovely goat
in plexiglass nor the elk shot
in the middle of a joke, but honest drunks,
crossed swords above the bar, three men hung
in the bad painting, others riding off
on the phony green horizon. The owner,
fresh from orphan wars, loves too
but bad as you. He keeps improving things
but can't cut the bodies down.

You need never leave. Money or a story
brings you booze. The elk is grinning
and the goat says go so tenderly
you hear him through the glass. If you weep
deer heads weep. Sing and the orphange
announces plans for your release. A train
goes by and ditches jump. You were nothing
going in and now you kiss your hand.

When mills shut down, when the worst drunk
says finally I'm stone, three men still hang
painted badly from a leafless tree, you
one of them, brains tied behind your back,
swinging for your sin. Or you swing
with goats and elk. Doors of orphanages
finally swing out and here you open in.

St. Ignatius Where the Salish Wail

It's a bad Good Friday, snow and mud
and mongrels in the road. Today's sky said
He'd weigh a ton tonight. A priest
unhooks the hands while Flatheads chant
ninety pounds of spices on the skin.
Another One, not the one they took down from
the cross, is lugged by six old Indians
around the room, five following with songs.

On a real Good Friday, warm and moon,
they'd pack Him outside where bright
fires burn. Here or there, the dialect
burns on their tongues. Elbow joints enflame
and still they crawl
nailed hours to the tomb. For men
who raced young April clouds and won, the pace
of reverence is grim. Their chanting
bangs the door of any man's first cave.

Mongrels have gone home. We slop
toward the car. Every year
a few less live who know the Salish hymns.
The mud is deeper. Snow has turned to rain.
We were renegade when God had gills.
We never change. Still, the raw sound
of their faces and the wailing unpretentious
color of their shawls——

Dog Lake With Paula

Snow air in the wind. It stings our lunch sacks,
arcs the nylon line. Being from the farm
you can take forever in your wild face
the boredom of wind across the boring glare.
On the farm, it's wheat. Here, water. Same.
Same blinding. Same remorseless drive
of yesterday and dream. A car starts
on the moon and suffocating caves
the mountain lion leaves are castle halls.

This wind is saying things it said at home.
Paula, go upwind to spawn, years across
the always slanted buffalo grass
and centuries past wheels that mill the water.
Deep in the Bear Tooth range the source of wind
is pulsing like your first man in the wheat.
It's not a source of wisdom. It's a wise mistake.
The wise result: pain of hungry horses,
howl of wild dogs in the blow. You swim upwind
so hard you have become the zany trees.

Look away when the lake glare hurts. Now,
look back. The float is diving. Deep down,
deeper than the lake, a trout is on the line.
We are, we always were, successful dogs.
Prehistoric beaches burn each dawn for loners.
Listen, Paula. Feel. This wind has traveled

all the way around the world, picked up heat
from the Sahara, a new Tasmanian
method of love, howl of the arctic whale.

Silver Star

This is the final resting place of engines,
farm equipment and that rare, never more
than occasional man. Population:
17. Altitude: unknown. For no
good reason you can guess, the woman
in the local store is kind. Old steam trains
have been rusting here so long, you feel
the urge to oil them, to lay new track, to start
the west again. The Jefferson
drifts by in no great hurry on its way
to wed the Madison, to be a tributary
of the ultimately dirty brown Missouri.
This town supports your need to run alone.

What if you'd lived here young, gone full of fear
to that stark brick school, the cruel teacher
supported by your guardian? Think well
of the day you ran away to Whitehall.
Think evil of the cop who found you starving
and returned you, siren open, to the house
you cannot find today. You question
everyone you see. The answer comes back wrong.
There was no house. They never heard your name.

When you leave here, leave in a flashy car
and wave goodbye. You are a stranger
every day. Let the engines and the farm
equipment die, and know that rivers

end and never end, lose and never lose
their famous names. What if your first girl
ended certain she was animal, barking
at the aides and licking floors? You know
you have no answers. The empty school
burns red in heavy snow.

With Kathy in Wisdom

I only dreamed that high cliff we were on
overlooking Wisdom and the Big Hole drain.
I dreamed us high enough to not see men,
dreamed old land behind us better left
and we were vagabond.

We went twice to Wisdom, not in dream.
Once in day, odd couple after Brooks,
and then at night, dark derelicts
obsessed with fake
false fronts for tourists and the empty church.

I dream the cliff again. Evening. Deep
beneath, Wisdom turning lights on. Neon flakes
are planets when we touch.
I wake up shouting, Wisdom's not that much,
and sweating. Wisdom never will be bright.

Lord, we need sun. We need moon. Fern
and mercy. Form and dream destroyed.
Need the cliff torn down. To hold hands
and stare down the raw void of the day.
Be my contraband.

Three fat Eastern Brook a night, that's
my private limit. The cliff broke
and wind pours in on Wisdom
leaving false fronts really what they seem.
Morning Wisdom, Kathy. It is no dream.

Indian Graves at Jocko

These dirt mounds make the dead seem fat.
Crude walls of rock that hold the dirt
when rain rides wild, were placed with skill
or luck. No crucifix can make
the drab boards of this chapel Catholic.
A mass across these stones becomes
whatever wail the wind decides is right.

They asked for, got the Black Robe
and the promised masses, well meant
promises, shabby third hand crosses.
This graveyard can expand, can crawl
in all directions to the mountains,
climb the mountains to the salmon
and a sun that toned the arrows
when animals were serious as meat.

The dead are really fat, the houses lean
from lack of loans. The river runs
a thin bed down the useless flat
where Flathead homes are spaced like friends.
The dead are strange
jammed this familial. A cheap fence
separates the chapel from the graves.

A forlorn lot like this, where snow
must crawl to find the tribal stones,
is more than just a grim result of cheat,

Garfield's forgery, some aimless trek
of horses from the stolen Bitter Root.
Dead are buried here because the dead
will always be obscure, wind
the one thing whites will always give a chance.

Drums in Scotland

Trumpets. A valley opens and beyond
the valley, closed and open sea. This land
is tough north music. Green cannot hide
the rock it hides and if horizon softens
into roll, it is the terrible drums
you dream are rolling. It is a curved sword
carving gray. It is counter roll
to rolling sky. And you were never wanted.

Rain. Small windows muting light until
the living room was dull, a hunger
that would go on hunger for the girl.
No warmth in eyes, arms, anything
but words. No warmth in words. The cat
kept staring and the woman in the kitchen
banged about. What good words were you saying
that the small girl listened? You walked
two miles to visit every Sunday and she
always said come in. No invitation
needed in the country. You just went and lied.

That's a long sky there from Scotland.
Same gray. Same relentless drive
of sky and music. It is your dream,
that terrible rolling drum. You were never
wanted and she always said come in.

Chysauster

Only these stone hut walls record their lives.
We know: not Roman. We speculate them
pastoral and kind. We say the grass is modern
but this gross wind must have been here then
tearing their eyes like ours, blurring the enemy
that never comes. And without trees no love
was secret on this hill. Your hot glance
at a girl exposed you to the grunting god
they hid with cattle in the far hut you were not
allowed to see. Where did they suddenly go,
third century, before Penzance and the discovery
of tin? You have to shout your theory
in this wind and shouted it sounds silly.
Black plague comes back laughter and grass bends
obedient as ancient beets. The size of huts
implies big families or people so communal
they did not use names. No one's found a coin,
something that might indicate exchange.
You loved your sister and she mocked you
as you crawled the dirt toward her, your breathing
muffled by her cackle and the drumming sky.

Montgomery Hollow

Birds here should have names so hard to say
you name them over. They finally found
the farmer hanging near the stream.
Only insect hum today and the purple odor
of thyme. You'd bet your throat against
the way a mind goes bad. You conquer loss
by going to the place it happened
and replaying it, saying the name
of the face in the open casket right.

People die in cities. Unless it's war
you never see the bodies. They die in print,
over phones in paramouric flats.
Here, you find them staring down the sun,
flies crawling them like bacon. Wives
scream two days running and the pain is gone.
Here, you find them living.

To know a road you own it, every bend
and pebble and the weeds along it,
dust that itches when the August hayrake
rambles home. You own the home.
You own the death of every bird you name.
To live good, keep your life and the scene.
Cow, brook, hay: these are names of coins.

Shark Island

Sun in our sails, our hooker wheels again
and again through the pollack school.
Our radio sends music through the village
you find sad, nine gray homes deserted
and no P.O. We toast our heavy catch
with stout. We lean back under a sky
wide as spread arms, sparkling with scales.
We are transported by our captain's hand
and breeze, are free and feel it under
those tortured rocks that tower and plunge
deep in green compounded by depth.
We are sailing an ocean and young.

The village nags. It dips and climbs, curves
by every pass we make through pollack
and it dies each time we see it. Where
are they? Were they happy? Did it hurt
to leave? We might grow old here, feed on
light from water and simple events—
the weekly boat with food from Bofin,
waving at hookers, pointing mute directions
on a noisy day. We might fake wisdom:
we have lived here long and understand
the urge to nothing, to a life inside.

Isn't it better, this wheeling, this sun
in our sails and the radio playing,
again and again through the school

with our greed. Monks get odd,
and without fans, hermits rage in caves.
Better to head for a loud port
where homes are loaded and the mail arrives.

Crinan Canal

There was never danger in this black sad water.
Not one monster. Not one cruel event along
the bank. It was peaceful even when that carnage
raged up north. The plague passed by
without one victim, and if a barge
hauled contraband, the tedious rhythm
of its cruise always made the mean cop sleep.
The captain of the tug arrived from upstream country
angry: they still sing about the girl
who threw the lock gate open at the curve.

The danger is the world reflected off the black.
The peace of maple shade is doubled. Silence
is compounded until wrens are roaring
and the soft plunk of a frog goes off
beside us bang. Fields that never meant
a lover harm slant eerie, and the next town
promises no language or a stove.

We have followed and followed it down,
past farm and kiln, the seldom used repair shop,
the warm creak of rusted lock gate gears,
unattended locks and wild vines thick
as the quiet, and here's the end: the town
and stores sell candy. The final gate swings open.
The black canal turns generous and green
and issues gifts, barges, tugs and sailboats
to the open world. Never was a danger
and they float out, foam out, sail out, loud.

The Lady in Kicking Horse Reservoir

Not my hands but green across you now.
Green tons hold you down, and ten bass curve
teasing in your hair. Summer slime
will pile deep on your breast. Four months of ice
will keep you firm. I hope each spring
to find you tangled in those pads
pulled not quite loose by the spillway pour,
stars in dead reflection off your teeth.

Lie there lily still. The spillway's closed.
Two feet down most lakes are common gray.
This lake is dark from the black blue Mission range
climbing sky like music dying Indians once wailed.
On ocean beaches, mystery fish
are offered to the moon. Your jaws go blue.
Your hands start waving every wind.
Wave to the ocean where we crushed a mile of foam.

We still love there in thundering foam
and love. Whales fall in love with gulls
and tide reclaims the Dolly skeletons
gone with a blast of aching horns to China.
Landlocked in Montana here
the end is limited by light, the final note
will trail off at the farthest point we see,
already faded, lover, where you bloat.

All girls should be nicer. Arrows rain
above us in the Indian wind. My future

should be full of windy gems, my past
will stop this roaring in my dreams.
Sorry. Sorry. Sorry. But the arrows sing:
no way to float her up. The dead sink
from dead weight. The Mission range
turns this water black late afternoons.

One boy slapped the other. Hard.
The slapped boy talked until his dignity
dissolved, screamed a single 'stop'
and went down sobbing in the company pond.
I swam for him all night. My only suit
got wet and factory hands went home.
No one cared the coward disappeared.
Morning then: cold music I had never heard.

Loners like work best on second shift.
No one liked our product and the factory closed.
Off south, the bison multiply so fast
a slaughter's mandatory every spring
and every spring the creeks get fat
and Kicking Horse fills up. My hope is vague.
The far blur of your bones in May
may be nourished by the snow.

The spillway's open and you spill out
into weather, lover down the bright canal
and mother, irrigating crops
dead Indians forgot to plant.
I'm sailing west with arrows to dissolving foam
where waves strand naked Dollys.
Their eyes are white as oriental mountains
and their tongues are teasing oil from whales.

Driving Montana

The day is a woman who loves you. Open.
Deer drink close to the road and magpies
spray from your car. Miles from any town
your radio comes in strong, unlikely
Mozart from Belgrade, rock and roll
from Butte. Whatever the next number,
you want to hear it. Never has your Buick
found this forward a gear. Even
the tuna salad in Reedpoint is good.

Towns arrive ahead of imagined schedule.
Absorakee at one. Or arrive so late—
Silesia at nine—you recreate the day.
Where did you stop along the road
and have fun? Was there a runaway horse?
Did you park at that house, the one
alone in a void of grain, white with green
trim and red fence, where you know you lived
once? You remembered the ringing creek,
the soft brown forms of far off bison.
You must have stayed hours, then drove on.
In the motel you know you'd never seen it before.

Tomorrow will open again, the sky wide
as the mouth of a wild girl, friable
clouds you lose yourself to. You are lost
in miles of land without people, without

100

one fear of being found, in the dash
of rabbits, soar of antelope, swirl
merge and clatter of streams.

Montana Ranch Abandoned

Cracks in eight log buildings, counting sheds
and outhouse, widen and a ghost peeks out.
Nothing, tree or mountain, weakens wind
coming for the throat. Even wind must work
when land gets old. The rotting wagon tongue
makes fun of girls who begged to go to town.
Broken brakerods dangle in the dirt.

Alternatives were madness or a calloused moon.
Wood they carved the plowblade from
turned stone as nameless gray. Indifferent flies
left dung intact. One boy had to leave
when horses pounded night, and miles away
a neighbor's daughter puked. Mother's cry
to dinner changed to caw in later years.

Maybe raiding bears or eelworms made them quit,
or daddy died, or when they planted wheat
dead Flatheads killed the plant. That stove
without a grate can't warm the ghost.
Tools would still be good if cleaned, but mortar
flakes and log walls sag. Even if you shored,
cars would still boom by beyond the fence, no glance
from drivers as you till the lunar dust.

Missoula Softball Tournament

This summer, most friends out of town
and no wind playing flash and dazzle
in the cottonwoods, music of the Clark Fork stale,
I've gone back to the old ways of defeat,
the softball field, familiar dust and thud,
pitcher winging drops and rises, and wives,
the beautiful wives in the stands, basic, used,
screeching runners home, infants unattended
in the dirt. A long triple sails into right center.
Two men on. Shouts from dugout: go, Ron, go.
Life is better run from. Distance to the fence,
both foul lines and dead center, is displayed.

I try to steal the tricky manager's signs.
Is hit-and-run the pulling of the ear?
The ump gives pitchers too much low inside.
Injustice? Fraud? Ancient problems focus
in the heat. Bad hop on routine grounder.
Close play missed by the team you want to win.
Players from the first game, high on beer,
ride players in the field. Their laughter
falls short of the wall. Under lights, the moths
are momentary stars, and wives, the beautiful wives
in the stands now take the interest they once feigned,
oh, long ago, their marriage just begun, years
of helping husbands feel important just begun,
the scrimping, the anger brought home evenings
from degrading jobs. This poem goes out to them.

Is steal-of-home the touching of the heart?
Last pitch. A soft fly. A can of corn
the players say. Routine, like mornings,
like the week. They shake hands on the mound.
Nice grab on that shot to left. Good game. Good game.
Dust rotates in their headlight beams.
The wives, the beautiful wives are with their men.

Hot Springs

You arrived arthritic for the cure,
therapeutic qualities of water
and the therapeutic air. Twenty-five
years later you limp out of bars
hoping rumors will revive, some doctor
will discover something curative
in natural steam. You have a choice
of abandoned homes to sleep in.
Motels constructed on the come
went broke before the final board
was nailed. Operative still:
your tainted fantasy and the delux hotel.

You have ached taking your aches up the hill.
Another battery of tests. Terrible probe
of word and needle. Always the fatal word—
when we get old we crumble. They wave
from the ward and you creak back down
to streets with wide lots between homes.
When that rare tourist comes, you tell him
you're not forlorn. There are advantages here—
easy pace of day, slow circle of sun.

If some day a cure's announced, for instance
the hot springs work, you will walk young
again in Spokane, find startling women,
you wonder why you feel empty and frown
and why goodbyes are hard. You go out healthy

on the gray thin road and when you look back
no one is waving. They kept no record
of your suffering, wouldn't know you
if you returned, without your cane, your grin.

Bear Paw

The wind is 95. It still pours from the east
like armies and it drains each day of hope.
From any point on the surrounding rim,
below, the teepees burn. The wind
is infantile and cruel. It cries 'give in' 'give in'
and Looking Glass is dying on the hill.
Pale grass shudders. Cattails beg and bow.
Down the draw, the dust of anxious horses
hides the horses. When it clears, a car
with Indiana plates is speeding to Chinook.

That bewildering autumn, the air howled
garbled information and the howl of coyotes
blurred the border. Then a lull in wind.
V after V of Canada geese. Silence
on the highline. Only the eternal nothing
of space. This is Canada and we are safe.
You can study the plaques, the unique names
of Indians and bland ones of the whites,
or study books, or recreate from any point
on the rim the action. Marked stakes tell you
where they fell. Learn what you can. The wind
takes all you learn away to reservation graves.

If close enough to struggle, to take blood
on your hands, you turn your weeping face
into the senile wind. Looking Glass is dead
and will not die. The hawk that circles overhead

is starved for carrion. One more historian
is on the way, his cloud on the horizon.
Five years from now the wind will be 100,
full of Joseph's words and dusting plaques.
Pray hard to weather, that lone surviving god,
that in some sudden wisdom we surrender.

Degrees of Gray in Philipsburg

You might come here Sunday on a whim.
Say your life broke down. The last good kiss
you had was years ago. You walk these streets
laid out by the insane, past hotels
that didn't last, bars that did, the tortured try
of local drivers to accelerate their lives.
Only churches are kept up. The jail
turned 70 this year. The only prisoner
is always in, not knowing what he's done.

The principal supporting business now
is rage. Hatred of the various grays
the mountain sends, hatred of the mill,
The Silver Bill repeal, the best liked girls
who leave each year for Butte. One good
restaurant and bars can't wipe the boredom out.
The 1907 boom, eight going silver mines,
a dance floor built on springs—
all memory resolves itself in gaze,
in panoramic green you know the cattle eat
or two stacks high above the town,
two dead kilns, the huge mill in collapse
for fifty years that won't fall finally down.

Isn't this your life? That ancient kiss
still burning out your eyes? Isn't this defeat
so accurate, the church bell simply seems
a pure announcement: ring and no one comes?

Don't empty houses ring? Are magnesium
and scorn sufficient to support a town,
not just Philipsburg, but towns
of towering blondes, good jazz and booze
the world will never let you have
until the town you came from dies inside?

Say no to yourself. The old man, twenty
when the jail was built, still laughs
although his lips collapse. Someday soon,
he says, I'll go to sleep and not wake up.
You tell him no. You're talking to yourself.
The car that brought you here still runs.
The money you buy lunch with,
no matter where it's mined, is silver
and the girl who serves your food
is slender and her red hair lights the wall.

from *What Thou Lovest
Well Remains American* (1975)

A Snapshot of the Auxiliary

In this photo, circa 1934,
you see the women of the St. James Lutheran
Womens Auxiliary. It is easy
to see they are German, short, squat,
with big noses, the sadness of the Dakotas
in their sullen mouths. These are exceptions:
Mrs. Kyte, English, who hated me.
I hated her and her husband.
Mrs. Noraine, Russian, kind. She saved me once
from a certain whipping. Mrs. Hillborn,
Swedish I think. Cheerful. Her husband
was a cop. None of them seem young. Perhaps
the way the picture was taken. Thinking back
I never recall a young face, a pretty one.
My eyes were like this photo. Old.

This one is Grandmother. This my Aunt Sarah,
still living. That one—I forget her name—
the one with maladjusted sons. That gray
in the photo was actually their faces.
On gray days we reflected weather color.
Lutherans did that. It made us children of God.
That one sang so loud and bad, I blushed.
She believed she believed the words.
She turned me forever off hymns. Even
the good ones, the ones they founded jazz on.

Many of them have gone the way wind recommends
or, if you're religious, God. Mrs. Noraine,

thank the wind, is alive. The church
is brick now, not the drab board frame
you see in the background. Once I was alone
in there and the bells, the bells started to ring.
They terrified me home. This next one in the album
is our annual picnic. We are all having fun.

Saying Goodbye to Mrs. Noraine

And after forty years her flowers failed to sing.
Geraniums blanched. Her blue begonias lost
their battle to the dulling rain. The neighborhood
was dead and gone. Only lines of kindness
in her face remained and her remarkable
arbor, my thoughts of wine. I stood clumsy
on her porch and worried if she wondered
why I'd come. When I walked in her door
I knew more secrets than ever about time.

It turned out I remembered most things wrong.
Miss Holy Roller never had
an illegitimate son. The military father
had been good to animals and the Gunthers
were indifferent to Hitler when we stoned
their house. I remembered some things right.
A dog was scalded by hot paraffin.
Two children died and a strange man really lived
alone a block away, shades always drawn,
and when we sang our mocking song about
the unseen man, we really heard him beating walls.

The rest was detail I had missed. Her husband's
agonizing prolonged death. Her plan to live
her last years in another city south.
It was lucky you came, she said. Four days
and I'll be gone. Outside, on the road
the city'd never paved, gravel cracked like popcorn

and everywhere the dandelions adult years
had taught me to ignore told me what I knew
when I was ten. Their greens are excellent
in salad. Their yellow flowers
make good wine and play off like a tune
against salal I love remembering to hum.

Flying, Reflying, Farming

We are flying white air. The most pioneering
falcon of all is hopelessly beneath us.
Nothing above but sky bleached out
by the sun's remorseless hammering
through ozone. Our lives inch back below,
the farm gray because a cruel past, weather
or mother, turns the spirit gray. The oldest
daughter left one day for good. The first son
(how can I know this at this altitude)
is trapped for life. At best, he can only get rich.
What good reason could the pilot have
for suddenly pointing the plane at the sun
and cutting the power? I hear his
hysterical laughter all the air down
to rock. We implode into acres
of black we rehearsed every young rage.
Another farm, tiny as the attendant's voice
on the defective intercom slips back
beneath us, bright orange this time and home.
We are flying white air.

The aluminum creaks. The wing shudders.
We are flying rough air. Remember
the wing snapping back over Europe
(where was that?), the agonizing sheer
you saw in slow motion, the vomit
you held back with prayer, and your friend
spinning down fatal ether

man had no business in. Back at the base
you were sobbing fields away from the rest
and the shepherd in black offered you pears
and wouldn't take your money. You claimed
you paid him with tears but that made no sense.
The air is solid again. We eat our way north.
We are flying good air.

We have entered the pattern.
Power reduced. Flaps down. Seat belt sign on.
In a moment, no smoking. This is always
a major kind of return. Thirty years ago
we came down and laughed and shook hands
after a rough one. We congratulated ourselves
for being alive. Long before that
we were ignorant farmers. Remember the night
you came home cheated in town of the money
you'd saved to paint the farm green.
Your wife called you weak and you stammered
and wept. Late one morning years later,
drunk and alone, you remembered above us
air is white, and you knew your next wife
would forgive you, your crops come
fatter than clouds, old friends return.
We have landed on schedule. Reverse thrust.
We are safe. We are natural on earth.

Last Day There

All furniture's gone. It hits me in this light
I've always hated thinned the way it is
by tiny panes, when I leave now the door will slam
no matter how I close it and my groin will throb
hungry as these rooms. Someone left the snapshot
on the wall, two horses and a man, a barn
dark gray against gray light I think was sky
but could be eighty years of fading. Once I called
that unknown farmer friend. He stared back
ignorant and cold until I blushed.
What denies me love today helps me hold a job.

This narrow space I slept in twenty years,
a porch walled in, a room just barely added on.
I own this and I know it is not mine.
That day I found locked doors in Naples, streets
rocked in the sea. The sea rocked in the hands
of brutal sky and fish came raining from volcanoes.
I see the horses swirl into the barn. I hear
two shots, no groans. When I say I'm derelict
the horses will return to flank the farmer.
Again, the three die gray as April 7, 1892.

I'll leave believing we keep all we lose and love.
Dirt roads are hard to find. I need to walk one
shabby some glamorous way the movies like.
I'll rest at creeks. I can't help looking deep
for trout in opaque pools. I pass a farm:

it's home, eviction papers posted to the door,
inside a fat ghost packing wine to celebrate
his fear of quarantine, once outside, pleased the road
he has to take goes north without an exit ramp,
not one sign giving mileage to the end.

What Thou Lovest Well Remains American

You remember the name was Jensen. She seemed old
always alone inside, face pasted gray to the window,
and mail never came. Two blocks down, the Grubskis
went insane. George played rotten trombone
Easter when they flew the flag. Wild roses
remind you the roads were gravel and vacant lots
the rule. Poverty was real, wallet and spirit,
and each day slow as church. You remember threadbare
church groups on the corner, howling their faith
at stars, and the violent Holy Rollers
renting that barn for their annual violent sing
and the barn burned down when you came back from war.
Knowing the people you knew then are dead,
you try to believe these roads paved are improved,
the neighbors, moved in while you were away, good-looking,
their dogs well fed. You still have need
to remember lots empty and fern.
Lawns well trimmed remind you of the train
your wife took one day forever, some far empty town,
the odd name you never recall. The time: 6:23.
The day: October 9. The year remains a blur.
You blame this neighborhood for your failure.
In some vague way, the Grubskis degraded you
beyond repair. And you know you must play again
and again Mrs. Jensen pale at her window, must hear
the foul music over the good slide of traffic.
You loved them well and they remain, still with nothing
to do, no money and no will. Loved them, and the gray

121

that was their disease you carry for extra food
in case you're stranded in some odd empty town
and need hungry lovers for friends, and need feel
you are welcome in the secret club they have formed.

Goodbye, Iowa

Once more you've degraded yourself on the road.
The freeway turned you back in on yourself
and you found nothing, not even a good false name.
The waitress mocked you and you paid your bill
sweating in her glare. You tried to tell her
how many lovers you've had. Only a croak came out.
Your hand shook when she put hot coins in it.
Your face was hot and you ran face down to the car.

Miles you hated her. Then you remembered what
the doctor said: really a hatred of self. Where
in flashes of past, the gravestone
you looked for years and never found, was there
a dignified time? Only when alone,
those solitary times with sky gray as a freeway.

And now you are alone. The waitress
will never see you again. You often pretend
you don't remember people you do. You joke back
spasms of shame from a night long ago.
Splintered glass. Bewildering blue swirl
of police. Light in your eyes. Hard questions.
Your car is cruising. You cross with ease
at 80 the state line and the state you are entering
always treated you well.

Farmer, Dying

Seven thousand acres of grass have faded yellow
from his cough. These limp days, his anger,
legend forty years from moon to Stevensville,
lives on, just barely, in a Great Falls whore.
Cruel times, he cries, cruel winds. His geese roam
unattended in the meadow. The gold last leaves
of cottonwoods ride Burnt Fork creek away.
His geese grow fat without him. Same old insult.
Same indifferent rise of mountains south,
hunters drunk around the fire ten feet from his fence.

What's killing us is something autumn. Call it
war or fever. You know it when you see it: flare.
Vine and fire and the morning deer come half
a century to sip his spring, there, at the far end
of his land, wrapped in cellophane by light.
What lives is what he left in air, definite,
unseen, hanging where he stood the day he roared.
A bear prowls closer to his barn each day.
Farmers come to watch him die. They bring crude offerings
of wine. Burnt Fork creek is caroling. He dies white
in final anger. The bear taps on his pane.

And we die silent, our last day loaded with the scream
of Burnt Fork creek, the last cry of that raging farmer.
We have aged ourselves to stone trying to summon
mercy for ungrateful daughters. Let's live him

in ourselves, stand deranged on the meadow rim
and curse the Baltic back, moon, bear and blast.
And let him shout from his grave for us.

Turtle Lake

The wind at Dog Lake whispered 'stranger' 'stranger'
and we drove away. When we dove down that hill
and flared out on the empty prairie, home seemed
less ashamed of us. My Buick hit a note too high
for dogs at 85 and cattails bowed like subjects
where we flashed through swamp. The wind died
back of us in slipstream. The sky kept chanting
'move like you are moved by water.' When we rolled
into Polson we were clean as kings.

Turtle is a lake the odd can own. It spreads
mercurial around those pastoral knolls.
The water waits so still, we listen to grim planets
for advice. The beat of trout hearts amplifies
against the Mission Range and when that throb returns
our faces glow the color of the lake. This
is where we change our names. Five clouds cross
the sun: the lake has been six colors,
counting that dejected gray our lives brought in.

The old man fishing fills his limit and goes home.
The heron takes his limit: one. All five clouds
poured east to oblivion and from the west advice
is pouring in. This mute wind
deeds the lake to us. Our homes have burned down
back where wind turned hungry friends away.
Whatever color water wants, we grant it with a wave.
We believe this luxury of bondage, the warm way
mountains call us citizens in debt.

Old Scene

All the essentials were there, the river thin
from distance in the canyon below, the house above
the canyon and the old man pruning trees. Whatever
he felt left out appeared, the carnival band
in step on the dirt road, the road remote enough
to need a name, lovely girls asking directions.
The old man's house was the last one. After that,
the road forever in the sun. He looked down that road
every noon and nothing came—mail or flashing girl.
He needed a dog but that you couldn't provide.

In time you gave him wisdom. A way of knowing
how things are from photos. He stared long enough
to make the photoed live. A farmer told him
pears grew big in '97. Children danced at dawn
and horses, the horses ran and ran. You let him
ride one and you helped him learn which woman
in one picture loved him at the Baptist fair.

You joined him one day at the river. After hours
of trout you walked together up the long slope
where he pointed to his house. He said 'Come in'
and built a fire and you said 'I live here too.'
Some days, the road fills suddenly with clowns.
The carnival band plays every tune you love.
Lovely girls stream in. You are dazzled
by their sequins, and the odor of their cooking
makes you laugh. Other days, the road hangs
empty. Not even birds can raise the dust.

Landscapes

If I painted, I'd paint landscapes. In museums
I stop often at van Ruysdael, and the wind he painted
high in European oaks gives license to my style.
I move the barn two feet. I curve the hill down
more dramatic. I put a woman on the hill against
the light, calling me to dinner. The wind I paint
is low and runs the grass down dancing to the sea.

In no time I have aged the barn stark gray.
Obviously, my cows hate no one. My wife
across the field stays carved out solid on the sky.
My tossed kiss stings her through the waves of heat
plowed dirt gives off in August. My tossed worm
drifts beneath the cutbank where I know trout wait.
As long as wind is pouring, my paint keeps farming green.

When wind stops, men come smiling with the mortgage.
They send me the eviction notice, postage due.
My cows are thin and failing. My deaf wife snarls
and claws the chair. The creek turns putrid.
I said fifty years moss on the roof is lovely.
It rots the roof. Oaks ache but cannot stir.
I call van Ruysdael from my knees on the museum floor.

In uniforms like yours you'll never understand.
Why these questions? The bank was wrong. The farm
is really mine. Even now along these pale green halls
I hear van Ruysdael's wind. Please know I rearranged things

only slightly, barn and hill. This is real: the home
that warps in August and the man inside who sold it
long ago, forgot he made the deal and will not move.

Iowa Déjà Vu

Did I come from this, a hardware store
in photos long ago? No customers.
No pleasures but the forced dream pike
are cruising hungry in the lake that glows
through oaks a small walk from the farm.
The church I must attend, hard dirt and plow,
sweating horse I swear at, all the hate
that makes today tomorrow.
Next farm down the daughters married Germans.
Girls don't like me in the town.

West of here love is opportune.
I get this from the soft cry of a train;
from magazines the barber lets me take.
West, it cools at night. Stars reproduce
like insects and wild horses sing.
Here it's planting time and never harvest,
nothing but the bitterest of picnics,
the camera just invented and in first prints
women faded and the children old.

Morning again. Morning forever. The heat
all night all day. The day of sweat
and heat forever and the train gone on.
It's where I began, first choking
on a promise to be nice, first dreaming pike
were hungry in the lake I didn't try.

The Freaks at Spurgin Road Field

The dim boy claps because the others clap.
The polite word, handicapped, is muttered in the stands.
Isn't it wrong, the way the mind moves back.

One whole day I sit, contrite, dirt, L.A.
Union Station, '46, sweating through last night.
The dim boy claps because the others clap.

Score, 5 to 3. Pitcher fading badly in the heat.
Isn't it wrong to be or not be spastic?
Isn't it wrong, the way the mind moves back.

I'm laughing at a neighbor girl beaten to scream
by a savage father and I'm ashamed to look.
The dim boy claps because the others clap.

The score is always close, the rally always short.
I've left more wreckage than a quake.
Isn't it wrong, the way the mind moves back.

The afflicted never cheer in unison.
Isn't it wrong, the way the mind moves back
to stammering pastures where the picnic should have worked.
The dim boy claps because the others clap.

Plans for Altering the River

Those who favor our plan to alter the river
raise your hand. Thank you for your vote.
Last week, you'll recall, I spoke about how water
never complains. How it runs where you tell it,
seemingly at home, flooding grain or pinched
by geometric banks like those in this graphic
depiction of our plan. We ask for power:
a river boils or falls to turn our turbines.
The river approves our plans to alter the river.

Due to a shipwreck downstream, I'm sad to report
our project is not on schedule. The boat
was carrying cement for our concrete rip rap
balustrade that will force the river to run
east of the factory site through the state-owned
grove of cedar. Then, the uncooperative
carpenters union went on strike. When we get
that settled, and the concrete, given good weather
we can go ahead with our plan to alter the river.

We have the injunction. We silenced the opposition.
The workers are back. The materials arrived
and everything's humming. I thank you
for this award, this handsome plaque I'll keep
forever above my mantle, and I'll read
the inscription often aloud to remind me
how with your courageous backing I fought

our battle and won. I'll always remember
this banquet this day we started to alter the river.

Flowers on the bank? A park on Forgotten Island?
Return of cedar and salmon? Who are these men?
These Johnnys-come-lately with plans to alter the river?
What's this wild festival in May
celebrating the runoff, display floats on fire
at night and a forest dance under the stars?
Children sing through my locked door, 'Old stranger,
we're going to alter, to alter, alter the river.'
Just when the water was settled and at home.

Three Stops to Ten Sleep

Ho. The horses can water. We are miles
ahead of schedule thanks to cool weather
and a strong wind at our backs. Ahead
are the mountains where we plan to build
our city. Our bank will be solvent. Our church
will serve all faiths. We will pass tough laws
against fragmentation. Anyone threatening
unity will be sent to the plains to wander
forever. The plains have snakes and wolves
and much of the water is poison. Have the women
make dinner. We camp here. Tomorrow
we should be close to that forest, and the next day
we will find our place to live as destined.

Stop. It is farther than it seemed. No doubt
an illusion created by light off high snow.
Then, the wind changed and discouraged
the horses. They don't like wind full in their eyes
all day. I urge you to stop this bickering.
Remember, our city will be founded
on mutual respect. I urge you to accept
this necessary rationing of food.
Above all, remember, every time you frown
the children see it. Several already
have been crying and saying there will be no city.

Wait. The mountains are never closer. What
is this land? We lost too many last night

in the storm and those who remain
are the worst, the ones we hesitated to take
when we started back at the river. You
remember? That town where we first formed?
Those saloons and loose women? Let them grumble.
We are going on. Indians know
the right roots to eat and there's water in cactus.
Even if we fail, wasn't it worth the trip,
leaving that corrupting music behind
and that sin?

The Art of Poetry

The man in the moon was better not a man.
Think, sad Raymond, how you glare across
the sea, hating the invisible near east
and your wife's hysteria. You'll always be here,
rain or gloom, painting a private Syria,
preferred dimensions of girls. Outside, gulls
scar across your fantasy. Rifled spray on glass
unfocuses the goats you stock on the horizon,
laddering blue like dolphins, looping over the sun.
Better the moon you need. Better not a man.
Sad Raymond, twice a day the tide comes in.

Envy your homemade heroes when the tide is low,
laughing their spades at clams, drinking a breezy beer
in breeze from Asia Minor, in those far far
principalities they've been, their tall wives elegant
in audience with kings. And envy that despairing man
you found one morning sobbing on a log,
babbling about a stuffed heart in Wyoming.
Don't think, Raymond, they'd respond to what's
inside you every minute, crawling slow as tide.
Better not tell them. Better the man you seem.
Sad Raymond, twice a night the tide comes in.

Think once how good you dreamed. The way you hummed
a melody from Norway when that summer storm
came battering the alders, turning the silver
underside of leaves toward the moon. And think,

sad Raymond, of the wrong way maturation came.
Wanting only those women you despised, imitating
the voice of every man you envied. The slow walk
home alone. Pause at door. The screaming kitchen.
And every day this window, loathing the real horizon.
That's what you are. Better the man you are.
Sad Raymond, twice a day the tide comes in.

All's in a name. What if you were Fred. Then none
of this need happen. What, sad Raymond, if
in your will you leave your tongue and tear ducts
to a transplant hospital. There's your motive
for trailing goats to Borneo, goats that suddenly
are real, outdistancing the quick shark
in the quarter mile and singing Home Sweet Home.
Motive, but no blood. Sad. Sad. The salty fusillade
obscures once more your raging playfield.
Better behind the glass. Better the man you were.
Sad Raymond, twice a night the tide comes in.

Sad Raymond, twice a lifetime the tyrant moon
loses control. Tides are run by starfish
and those charts you study mornings on your wall
are meaningless as tide. The near east isn't near
or east and Fred was an infant in your neighborhood
devoured by a dog. Those days you walk the beach
looking for that man who's pure in his despair.
He's never there. A real man walks the moon
and you can't see him. The moon is cavalier.
Better to search your sadness for the man.
Sad Raymond, twice a moment tides come in.

from *31 Letters and 13 Dreams* (1977)

Letter to Kizer from Seattle

Dear Condor: Much thanks for that telephonic support
from North Carolina when I suddenly went ape
in the Iowa tulips. Lord, but I'm ashamed.
I was afraid, it seemed, according to the doctor
of impending success, winning some poetry prizes
or getting a wet kiss. The more popular I got,
the softer the soft cry in my head: Don't believe them.
You were never good. Then I broke and proved it.
Ten successive days I alienated women
I liked best. I told a coed why her poems were bad
(they weren't) and didn't understand a word I said.
Really warped. The phrase "I'll be all right"
came out too many unsolicited times. I'm o.k. now.
I'm back at the primal source of poems: wind, sea
and rain, the market and the salmon. Speaking
of the market, they're having a vital election here.
Save the market? Tear it down? The forces of evil
maintain they're trying to save it too, obscuring,
of course, the issue. The forces of righteousness,
me and my friends, are praying for a storm, one
of those grim dark rolling southwest downpours
that will leave the electorate sane. I'm the last poet
to teach the Roethke chair under Heilman.
He's retiring after 23 years. Most of the old gang
is gone. Sol Katz is aging. Who isn't? It's close now
to the end of summer and would you believe it
I've ignored the Blue Moon. I did go to White Center,
you know, my home town, and the people there,
many are the same, but also aging, balding, remarkably
polite and calm. A man whose name escapes me
said he thinks he had known me, the boy who went alone

to Longfellow Creek and who laughed and cried
for no reason. The city is huge, maybe three quarters
of a million and lots of crime. They are indicting
the former chief of police. Sorry to be so rambling.
I eat lunch with J. Hillis Miller, brilliant and nice
as they come, in the faculty club, overlooking the lake,
much of it now filled in. And I tour old haunts,
been twice to Kapowsin. One trout. One perch. One poem.
Take care, oh wisest of condors. Love. Dick. Thanks again.

Letter to Matthews from Barton Street Flats

Dear Bill: This is where the Nisei farmed, here where the blacktop
of a vast shopping complex covers the rich black bottom land.
Lettuce sparkled like a lake. Then, the war took everything,
farm, farmers and my faith that change (I really mean loss)
is paced slow enough for the blood to adjust. I believed
the detention of Tada, my friend, was temporary madness
like the war. Someday, I thought, it will all be over, this
tearing out everything, this shifting people away like
so many pigs to single thickness walled shacks in Wyoming
where winter rips like the insane self-righteous tongue
of the times. In Germany, Jews. In America, Japs.
They came back and their property was gone, some technicality
those guardians of society, lawyers found. Or their goods
had burned in unexplained fires. Tada came back wounded
from honest German guns and got insulted in White Center—
I was with him—oh, a dreadful scene. He moved justly bitter
to Milwaukee. Haven't seen him in years. Why do I think
of this today? Why, faced with this supermarket parking lot
filled with gleaming new cars, people shopping unaware
a creek runs under them, do I think back thirty some years
to that time all change began, never to stop, not even
to slow down one moment for us to study our loss, to recall
the Japanese farmers bent deep to the soil? Hell, Bill,
I don't know. You know the mind, how it comes on the scene again
and makes tiny histories of things. And the imagination
how it wants everything back one more time, how it detests
all progress but its own, all war but the one it fights over
and over, the one no one dares win. And we can deport those
others and feel safe for a time, but old dangers (and pleasures)
return. And we return to the field of first games where,

143

when we find it again, we look hard for the broken toy,
the rock we called home plate, evidence to support our claim
our lives really happened. You can say this all better.
Please do. Write it the way it should sound. The gain will be mine.
Use my Montana address. I'm going back home, not bent
under the load of old crops, still fat and erect, still with faith
we process what grows to the end, the poem. Your good friend, Dick.

In Your War Dream

You must fly your 35 missions again.
The old base is reopened. The food is still bad.
You are disturbed. The phlegm you choked up
mornings in fear returns. You strangle on the phlegm.
You ask, "Why must I do this again?" A man
replies, "Home." You fly over one country
after another. The nations are bright like a map.
You pass over the red one. The orange one ahead
looks cold. The purple one north of that is the one
you must bomb. A wild land. Austere. The city
below seems ancient. You are on the ground.
Lovers are inside a cabin. You ask to come in.
They say "No. Keep watch on Stark Yellow Lake."
You stand beside the odd water. A terrible wind
keeps knocking you down. "I'm keeping watch
on the lake," you yell at the cabin. The lovers
don't answer. You break into the cabin. Inside
old women bake bread. They yell, "Return to the base."
You must fly your 35 missions again.

In Your Bad Dream

Morning at nine, seven ultra-masculine men
explain the bars of your cage are silver
in honor of our emperor. They finger the bars
and hum. Two animals, too far to name,
are fighting. One, you are certain, is destined
to win, the yellow one, the one who from here
seems shaped like a man. Your breakfast
is snake but the guard insists eel. You say hell
I've done nothing. Surely that's not a crime.
You say it and say it. When men leave, their hum
hangs thick in the air as scorn. Your car's
locked in reverse and running. The ignition
is frozen, accelerator stuck, brake shot.
You go faster and faster back. You wait for the crash.
On a bleak beach you find a piano the tide
has stranded. You hit it with a hatchet.
You crack it. You hit it again and music
rolls dissonant over the sand. You hit it
and hit it driving the weird music from it.
A dolphin is romping. He doesn't approve.
On a clean street you join the parade. Women
line the streets and applaud, but only the band.
You ask to borrow a horn and join in.
The bandmaster says we know you can't play.
You are embarrassed. You pound your chest
and yell meat. The women weave into the dark
that is forming, each to her home. You know
they don't hear your sobbing crawling the street
of this medieval town. You promise money
if they'll fire the king. You scream a last promise—
Anything. Anything. Ridicule my arm.

Letter to Mantsch from Havre

Dear Mike: We didn't have a chance. Our starter had no change
and second base had not been plugged since early in July.
How this town turned out opening night of the tournament
to watch their Valley Furniture team wipe us, the No-
Name Tavern of Missoula, out. Remember Monty Holden,
ace Havre pitcher, barber, hero of the Highline, and his
tricky "catch-this" windup? First inning, when you hit that shot,
one on, the stands went stone. It still rockets the night.
I imagine it climbing today, somewhere in the universe,
lovelier than a girl climbs on a horse and lovelier than star.
We lost that game. No matter. Won another. Lost again
and went back talking fondly of your four home runs,
triple and single in three games, glowing in the record book.
I came back after poems. They ask me today, here in Havre,
who's that player you brought here years ago, the hitter?
So few of us are good at what we do, and what we do,
well done or not, seems futile. I'm trying to find Monty
Holden's barber shop. I want to tell him style in anything,
pitching, hitting, cutting hair, is worth our trying even
if we fail. And when that style, the graceful compact swing
leaves the home crowd hearing its blood and the ball roars off
in night like determined moon, it is our pleasure
to care about something well done. If he doesn't understand
more than the final score, if he says, "After all, we won,"
I'll know my hair will not look right after he's done,
what little hair I have, what little time. And I'll drive home
knowing his windup was all show, glad I was there years back,
that I was lucky enough to be there when with one swing
you said to all of us, this is how it's done. The ball jumps
from your bat over and over. I want my poems to jump

like that. All poems. I want to say once to a world that feels
with reason it has little chance, well done. That's the lie
I cannot shout loud as this local truth: Well done, Mike. Dick.

Letter to Stafford from Polson

Dear Bill: We don't know the new heavy kind of wolf
killing calves, but we've seen it and it's anything but gray.
We have formed a new heavy kind of posse
and we're fanning the Mission range for unique tracks.
The new wolf is full of tricks. For instance, yesterday
he sat all afternoon in a bar disguised as a trout
and none of us caught on. He's a wily one.
He even went home drunk and of course weaving slow,
passed two cars of cops and the Union '76
the usually sharp reliable and somewhat sly one runs.
I guess we're not observant. Aside from the wolf
things go well. This is where you may recall you stood
looking at Flathead Lake and uttered a Stafford line.
Impressed by the expanse you said something about going
on and on. And that's exactly what we've done.
We have a new club called the South Shore Inn,
fair food, good drinks and a panoramic view
of the mountains and lake. Also a couple of posh motels
have been added, a new supermarket and in progress
a mooring harbor for yachts. I personally think
the wolf wants to be one of us, to give up killing
and hiding, the blue cold of the mountains, the cave
where he must live alone. I think he wants to come down
and be a citizen, swim, troll all summer for Mackinaws
and in autumn snag salmon. I have to close now.
The head of the posse just called and two more calves
with throats cut were found this morning one mile south
of the garbage dump. Our chief said this time
we'll get him. This time we plan to follow his howl
all the way to the source, even if it means scaling cliffs
and beating our way through snow. Why does he do it?

149

He doesn't eat what he kills. I hope we find out. I hope
he breaks and spills all the secrets of his world.
By the way, it turns out he's green with red diagonal stripes
and jitters in wind like a flag. Take care, Bill. Dick.

In Your Small Dream

A small town slanted on a slight hill
in barren land. First building you see:
red brick with oriental trim. You say,
"A unique building," and the road forks
into three. Road left, brief with old men
leaning on brick walls. They frown the sun away.
Middle road, oblique and long. Same red brick
buildings but without the trim. Same drab
roasting buildings. Young men and cafes.
You call it Main Street. The third road
you never see. You walk up Main Street.
You are hungry. You take this opportunity
to eat. You have no money. They throw you out.
You return to the brief street. You ask old men
"Where's the unique building?" They frown
and turn away. You say, "I am a friend."
You know wind will level this town.
You say, "Get out. The wind is on its way."
The old men frown. The day darkens. You look
hard for the third road. You ask a giant, "Where?"
The giant glowers, "The third road is severe."
You run and run. You cannot leave the town.

In Your Blue Dream

You are fishing a lake but so far no fish.
The other men fishing are old. They nod approval
of your rod, limber and green. One yells advice
over the lake: develop the eyes of an osprey.
The sun goes down. You row to the shore.
A warden is there. He arrests you. He says
your bait is illegal, live meat. The old men
pay your bail. You sweat when the girl counts the money.
The sky fills with fish hawks each with a trout
in his beak. The streets fill with men enroute home.
You lose your sense of time. You ask the men,
all young, is this afternoon? They don't answer.
You run from man to man asking the time.
You forget your address. You knock on a door.
A luscious blonde tells you you have the wrong town.
You run through the swamp. The town ahead
glitters warm in the dark. You yell at the town,
where is my home? A mob of men with bloodhounds
is back of you somewhere. You hear them. You rush
for the lights. You are in the streets dirty in rags.
The people are elegant, dressed for the clubs.
You show them your key. They answer firmly,
you have the wrong country. Go north. You sob
in the streets. You say, this, this is my land.
The streetlamps dim. A cop says, go home.
When the posse of women find you in the desert
you are terribly ashamed. You babble on and on.
They point at you and laugh. One says, you look good
bleaching, good for a weathered skeleton.

Letter to Scanlon from Whitehall

Dear Dennice: I'm this close but the pass is tough this year.
I'm stranded by this rotten winter. My car is ailing
and the local mechanic doesn't know what he's doing
or he does but never learned clear phrasing. It will take
four hours or a week. An odd town. A friendly waitress
says the main drag is the old road so I must have been here
but I don't remember. It looks like several towns
in Montana. Columbus, for one. Even, a little, like the edge
of Billings. You know. On one side, stores, cafes, a movie
theatre you feel certain no one attends. And across
the street, the railroad station. Most of all, that desolate
feeling you get, young hunger, on a gray sunday afternoon,
when you survive only because the desolation feeds
your dying, a dream of living alone on the edge
of a definite place, a desert or the final house in town
with no threat of expansion, or on the edge of a canyon,
coyotes prowling below and a wind that never dies. Girl,
you wouldn't believe the people who live alone, preparing
themselves daily for dying, planning their expenditures
to the penny so just when they die their money is gone
and the county must bury them, a final revenge on a world
that says work is good, plan for the future. They did. And dear
Dennice, bring their laughing bones no flowers. Pay them the honor
of ignoring their graves, the standard bird authorities
chip on stones, a magpie designed by the same man
you always see in towns like this, sitting in the station,
knowing the trains don't run. The soup in the cafe I was lucky
enough to pick of the available three, turned out thick
tomato macaroni, and the chicken salad sandwich, yum.
The mechanic says my car is done. He says, if I understand,
it's ready and no charge. He says, if I understand, he

just wants to be friendly and it wasn't anything really wrong.
Homestake grade is sanded. I may even beat this letter
to your home. It's saturday and I suppose there's a dance
somewhere in Butte tonight. Would you please consider?
Would you come? I hope it's one of those virtuoso bands,
you know, songs from all the generations, jazz, swing, rock.
And a big crowd. Girls in mini minis, tighter than skin
over their behinds, and a friendly bar, a table where
we can talk. Think about it. Say yes. Be nice. Love. Dick.

In Your Wild Dream

You are fishing but have walked away from your rod.
Your rod bends and flies into the lake. You swim
to the rod and start reeling in. A huge fish in on.
A gray fish. Bloated. Dull. You finally land him.
On shore he snarls, a vicious mustard dog.
He wants to kill you. He rages with hate and glares.
A man you don't know is holding him back.
The dog strains at the rope. The man says "a Girl fish,
that's what he's called." You are riding a camel
in Athens. The citizens yell, "We are not Arab. This
is not sand." The camel is a yacht. You cruise
a weird purple river. Girls doze on the bank. One
stands up and waves. You yell, "Where is the town?"
You are alone. Fishing again. You catch nothing.
You dream you are dreaming all this. Around you
beautiful flowers are blooming. You know now
you need nothing to live, food, love or water.
Youg giggle and giggle because you are free.
Birds above you keep flying away.

Letter to Levertov from Butte

Dear Denise: Long way from, long time since Boulder. I hope
you and Mitch are doing OK. I get rumors. You're in Moscow,
Montreal. Whatever place I hear, it's always one of glamor.
I'm not anywhere glamorous. I'm in a town where children
get hurt early. Degraded by drab homes. Beaten by drunken
parents, by other children. Mitch might understand. It's kind
of a microscopic Brooklyn, if you can imagine Brooklyn
with open pit mines, and more Irish than Jewish. I've heard
from many of the students we had that summer. Even seen
a dozen or so since then. They remember the conference fondly.
So do I. Heard from Herb Gold twice and read now and then
about Isaac Bashevis Singer who seems an enduring diamond.
The mines here are not diamond. Nothing is. What endures
is sadness and long memories of labor wars in the early
part of the century. This is the town where you choose sides
to die on, company or man, and both are losers. Because
so many people died in mines and fights, early in history
man said screw it and the fun began. More bars and whores
per capita than any town in America. You live only
for today. Let me go symbolic for a minute: great birds
cross over you anyplace, here they grin and dive. Dashiell
Hammett based *Red Harvest* here though he called it Personville
and "person" he made sure to tell us was "poison" in the slang.
I have ambiguous feelings coming from a place like this
and having clawed my way away, thanks to a few weak gifts
and psychiatry and the luck of living in a country
where enough money floats to the top for the shipwrecked
to hang on. On one hand, no matter what my salary is
or title, I remain a common laborer, stained by the perpetual
dust from loading flour or coal. I stay humble, inadequate
inside. And my way of knowing how people get hurt, make

156

my (damn this next word) heart go out through the stinking air
into the shacks of Walkerville, to the wife who has turned
forever to the wall, the husband sobbing at the kitchen
table and the unwashed children taking it in and in and in
until they are the wall, the table, even the dog the parents
kill each month when the money's gone. On the other hand,
I know the cruelty of poverty, the embittering ways
love is denied, and food, the mean near-insanity of being
and being deprived, the trivial compensations of each day,
recapturing old years in broadcast tunes you try to recall
in bars, hunched over the beer you can't afford, or bending
to the bad job you're lucky enough to have. How, finally,
hate takes over, hippie, nigger, Indian, anyone you can lump
like garbage in a pit, including women. And I don't want
to be part of it. I want to be what I am, a writer good enough
to teach with you and Gold and Singer, even if only in
some conference leader's imagination. And I want my life
inside to go on long as I do, though I only populate bare
landscape with surrogate suffering, with lame men
crippled by more than disease, and create finally
a simple grief I can deal with, a pain the indigent can find
acceptable. I do go on. Forgive this raving. Give my best
to Mitch and keep plenty for yourself. Your rich friend, Dick.

Letter to Kathy from Wisdom

My dearest Kathy: When I heard your tears and those of your
mother over the phone from Moore, from the farm
I've never seen and see again and again under the most
uncaring of skies, I thought of this town I'm writing from,
where we came lovers years ago to fish. How odd
we seemed to them here, a lovely young girl and a fat
middle 40's man they mistook for father and daughter
before the sucker lights in their eyes flashed on. That was
when we kissed their petty scorn to dust. Now, I eat alone
in the cafe we ate in then, thinking of your demons, the sad
days you've seen, the hospitals, doctors, the agonizing
breakdowns that left you ashamed. All my other letter
poems I've sent to poets. But you, your soft round form
beside me in our bed at Jackson, you were a poet then,
curving lines I love against my groin. Oh, my tenderest
racoon, odd animal from nowhere scratching for a home,
please believe I want to plant whatever poem will grow
inside you like a decent life. And when the wheat you've known
forever sours in the wrong wind and you smell it
dying in those acres where you played, please know
old towns we loved in matter, lovers matter, playmates, toys,
and we take from our lives those days when everything moved,
tree, cloud, water, sun, blue between two clouds, and moon,
days that danced, vibrating days, chance poem. I want one
who's wondrous and kind to you. I want him sensitive
to wheat and how wheat bends in cloud shade without wind.
Kathy, this is the worst time of day, nearing five, gloom
ubiquitous as harm, work shifts changing. And our lives
are on the line. Until we die our lives are on the mend.
I'll drive home when I finish this, over the pass that's closed
to all but a few, that to us was always open, good days

years ago when our bodies were in motion and the road rolled out
below us like our days. Call me again when the tears build
big inside you, because you were my lover and you matter,
because I send this letter with my hope, my warm love. Dick.

In Your Big Dream

Though alone, you know just over the hill
the army is ready. You decide, if they come,
you'll say you support their cause. You dwell
in the ruins of a church. A bird you know's
ferocious circles the church. You see him
through the huge gaps in the roof. You pull
the bellrope thinking clang will drive him away.
But will it attract the army? You are free
from gravity. You lift five feet off the ground
and glide. You decide to follow a river
all the way to the sea. People along the way
warn you, a monster's downstream. You walk
the streets of a deserted city. You know
it was deserted recently because the lights
still burn and markets display fresh meat.
If anyone comes, you'll say you're chief of police.
Enemy subs pop up on the sea. They shell
the coast. You wave your hair in surrender.
Only one man comes ashore, a small man.
He refuses your terms. He says it's not your land.
You whine. You beg him to take you prisoner.
Bison stampede the plain. You climb a mountain
leading seven men who look like you. They depend
on you for their safety. You climb higher
and higher until you are alone under a sun
gone pale in altitude. You climb above birds
and clouds. You are home in this atmosphere.

In Your Good Dream

From this hill they are clear, the people
in pairs emerging from churches, arm
in soft arm. And limb on green limb
the shade oaks lining the streets form
rainproof arches. All day festive tunes
explain your problems are over. You picnic
alone on clean lawn with your legend.
Girls won't make fun of you here.

Storms are spotted far off enough
to plan going home and home has fire.

It's been here forever. Two leisurely grocers
who never compete. At least ten elms
between houses and rapid grass refilling
the wild field for horses. The same mayor
year after year—no one votes anymore—
stocks bass in the ponds and monster trout
in the brook. Anger is outlawed.
The unpleasant get out. Two old policemen
stop children picking too many flowers
in May and give strangers directions.

You know they are happy. Best to stay
on the hill, drowsy witness, hearing
the music, seeing their faces beam
and knowing they marry forever, die late
and are honored in death. A local process,
no patent applied for, cuts name, born date
and died too deep in the headstone to blur.